Crib Notes for

THE

FIRST YEAR

OF

FATHERHOOD

Crib Notes for
THE
FIRST YEAR
OF
FATHERHOOD

A Survival Guide for New Fathers

Everett De Morier

Fairview Press
Minneapolis

Published by Fairview Press, 2450 Riverside Avenue South, Minneapolis, MN 55454.

Library of Congress Cataloging-in-Publication Data
De Morier, Everett, 1962-
    Crib notes for the first year of fatherhood : a survival guide for new fathers / Everett De Morier.
        p.   c.m.
    Includes bibliographical references and index.
    ISBN 1-57749-073-8
    1. Fatherhood. 2. Parenting.   I. Title.
HQ756.D4   1998
306.874'2--dc21   98-24290
                                                                           CIP

First Printing: September 1998
Printed in the United States of America
02 01 00 99 98   7 6 5 4 3 2 1

Cover design: Laurie Duren

Publisher's Note: The publications of Fairview Press, including *Crib Notes for the First Year of Fatherhood,* do not necessarily reflect the philosophy of Fairview Health Services.

For a free current catalog, call toll-free 1–800–544–8207, or visit our website at www.Press.Fairview.org.

To my sons Nicholas and Alexander,
who taught me that when things get crazy,
just spin in a circle until you get sick.

TABLE OF CONTENTS

ACKNOWLEDGMENTS

I would like to thank the following people who made this book possible:

Lane Stiles, Senior Editor at Fairview Press, who patiently taught me a great deal about writing and publishing and always had time for my stupid questions, no matter how busy he was.

Dan Verdick, Marketing Director at Fairview Press, who kept it fun and thought that his idea for a book about fatherhood was better than my idea for *Crib Notes for the First Year of Clog Dancing*.

To Ed Wright, who made the numbers in this book make sense.

To my wife, Debbie-Jean, for her help in the research as well as the fact that every day she doesn't divorce me is a testimonial to her perseverance.

And to my mom, who always taught me to keep my head in the clouds and worry about where my feet were later.

INTRODUCTION

If I think back, I can remember the time before Debbie and I had kids. The quiet time when our cupboards weren't toddler-proof, and when we didn't have to spell words because small ears were nearby. The time before Debbie's pregnancies, before she owned pants with elastic waists. The time when my family consisted of the two of us and the world's only hyperactive basset hound.

Although I don't actually remember thinking about it, we must have decided that we had entirely too much disposable time and money on our hands, and too many hours of REM sleep each night. Because suddenly, we were trying to have children.

That may sound silly. How could we be trying to do something people have been doing by accident for thousands of years? Still, we were trying, and there was no doubt that nothing was happening. We did not want to fail Reproduction and have to take Remedial Reproduction, which is taught in the summer.

So, we took the next logical step: we went to a doctor to find out what was wrong with us, or, more precisely, what was wrong with me.

Thus began my humiliating journey of tests and assignments, the least of which was wearing boxer shorts instead of briefs. Several months later, when the doctors were fairly confident that I had performed every ignominious act they could think of, I was certified 100 percent baby-making material. I even got a little certificate that Debbie lets me hang up downstairs near the furnace.

Of course, that was the good news. The bad news: it was now Debbie's turn for embarrassing tests. After thyroid medication, some very bizarre procreation practices, and a trip to Key West, we became pregnant.

Debbie told me not to tell anyone our secret until the first three months had gone by, but the mailman congratulated me the next day. (I guess the rule was that *I* was not to tell anyone.) Then it all began: the planning, the buying, the overeating (some of it done by Debbie), the crying (some also done by Debbie), and the waiting. The day finally came, and Nick was born.

Our world changed dramatically. Our routines changed, our budget changed, our free time changed, our sleep schedule changed, and our apartment changed. Debbie said she couldn't believe how hard it was, and that it was much more difficult than she had ever expected it to be. Me? I was too tired to talk.

But she was right. Before Nick, we didn't know what sleep deprivation did to the mind and body. We didn't know what croup was or how to treat it. We didn't know how to handle the stress of work and the stress of home, or how to be both a couple and part of a family. We weren't prepared for these things, so the first year was harder than we had thought it would be.

I remember thinking that it took years for Nick to sleep through the night (it took ten weeks). And then he crawled, walked, and talked. The first three years of his life seemed to take ten. And everyone told us not to worry; the second baby would be easier.

And he was. A great deal easier.

With Alex, our second child, we got more sleep. We were healthier and less frustrated. Had we produced a genetically superior child the second time, or did we just know what we were doing? I believe it was the latter. We knew what to expect, the tricks and the traps. We knew how to save money and how to schedule. We could confidently handle a newborn. I decided to describe what I had learned to other new fathers, along with the observations of experts in the field. *Crib Notes for the First Year of Fatherhood* offers insight into that first year, giving you the hints, suggestions, and resources on money, personal issues, relationships, family, and other concerns that new fathers have.

Because what happens in the first year of fatherhood?

Change.

Most of us hear that word and panic. We want things to remain the same, but to improve. Of course, we expect some change when the first child is born, but we are shocked when the event touches every area of our lives: our careers, our friendships, our leisure time, our relationships. Becoming a father is a life change, and few areas remain untouched.

It may be frightening to know that your entire life will change. But looking back, I can say that this change gave me a new appreciation for everyday life.

One hot summer day, when Nick was a baby, he and I sat in the living room blowing bubbles. The air conditioner was running in the dining room, and a fan in our living room circulated the cool air. The breeze from the fan lifted up the bubbles, sending them toward the dining room. The air conditioner sent them swirling back into the living room, where they were caught again by the movement of the fan. Nick and I sat on the carpet, mesmerized by a roomful of traveling rainbow bubbles.

That is one of the gifts of fatherhood: being able to experience childhood one more time. We can go to kindergarten, see the circus, learn to ride a bike, and explore *The Wizard of Oz* all over again. This is why we drive long distances and pay whatever we must so that our children can sit in a pool of colored plastic balls. Part of our willingness is for their happiness, and the rest is for ours. We can experience the excitement of childhood with the appreciation of an adult.

About the Crib Notes Series

SEVERAL YEARS AGO, as I stood on a ladder, cleaning the outside windows of our old apartment, I thought of all the changes that had occurred since Debbie and I first met. Although we'd been married two years by then, I realized we had changed the most during that first year, in terms of emotions and finances. We had become friends, a team, and a couple.

There on that ladder, under an ammonia-induced delirium, I decided to see if anyone had ever written a book about the first year of marriage—not a clinical study, but a light and goofy look at the changes that occur, with helpful hints and information on everything from finances to relationships to time and family. That concept evolved into *Crib Notes for the First Year of Marriage: A Survival Guide for Newlyweds.*

Getting married, of course, had a huge impact on my life, and so did becoming a father. That's why I wrote the second installment of the Crib Notes series. I hope you'll find it to be a light, informative view of what happens when you become a father. The goal is to give you ideas about what to expect and what to prepare for, and to direct you to resources that will make the change easier to bear and more enjoyable.

Exactly what is the father's job in the first year of fatherhood? Is he a husband, buddy, nursemaid, helper, supporter, teacher, body-guard? Yes, all of the above. If we know what to do as fathers in the first year, we'll be able to support the new mother, be helpful, get involved, and be aware of the physical and emotional changes that are occurring in all of us. Our role is to be ourselves. Our job is to accept our new position and begin training, learning, and having fun.

That's what this book is all about. In the following pages, you'll learn simple but important skills for remaining a couple while becoming a family. You'll learn how to deal with sleep deprivation, save on everything from diapers to daycare, divide up household responsibilities, and live on a budget. You'll find resources for more information, workbook pages to help you think on paper, and details that will save you time, money, and energy.

But in the meantime, if I haven't said it already, congratulations.

Congratulations on being a new father and a new person.

Congratulations on the opportunity to see the universe all over again, for the second time.

Congratulations on the excitement of beginning your new life and new family.

Congratulations.

♞ ZERO MINUS ONE, ♞ AND COUNTING

Malone: *"Do you know what a blood oath is, Mr. Ness?"*
Ness: *"Yes."*
Malone: *"Good. 'Cause you just took one."*
—The Untouchables

Month eight of the pregnancy: now, that's an exciting time for a father-to-be. That's when we officially move into yellow alert, the flurry of last minute preparations for the big day. In the eighth month of pregnancy, you and your partner will decide where to have the baby, and, if your destination is the local hospital or birthing room, you'll pack your bags. After that, there's not much more to do but wonder, worry, and wait—with the waiting part often being the hardest.

You wait for a sign that the real pain is about to begin. The mother-to-be has already suffered from nausea, weight gain, insomnia, swollen feet, and hormonal changes. Soon, it will be time for the contractions, labor, delivery, and recovery.

Fathers-to-be feel the pain, too. For example, if you, as labor coach, don't place your hand deeply enough in your partner's when a major contraction hits, there's a good chance that your five thin fingers will be fused into one fat one. Or, if you're sitting next to your partner, watching the monitor for the peak of the next contraction, you may say encouragingly for the sixty-third time, "Here comes another one. This is a tiny one. No big deal. Okay, small breaths." Don't be surprised if you hear her screech, "You wouldn't know a big contraction from a hangnail!" just before the room goes black. Later, as the emergency room staff removes the last piece of the desk lamp from your skull, you can rest assured that you've experienced a fraction of what labor pain feels like.

Just the same, thank your lucky stars that you'll be welcome in the delivery room. Not too many years ago, this would not have been allowed; doctors felt there was too much risk of infection to allow fathers to participate. That's why mothers-to-be were whisked away to the delivery room, while fathers-to-be paced in the waiting areas.

This started to change in October, 1964, when the California Board of Health allowed a father to be present in the delivery room for the first time. Not until 1974 did the American College of Obstetricians and Gynecologists support this move, and then, only after research showed that the mother and new baby were not exposed to unnecessary risk if the father was present at a normal delivery.

As a result, the doors to the delivery room opened wide. Now, you, too, can participate in one of the most wonderful miracles of life.

Locations for the Delivery

AS THE BIRTH draws nearer, plans for the delivery should be finalized. Where you plan to have your baby will depend on the pregnancy's level of risk and your own personal preferences. Talk to your physician or midwife before you decide which option will offer the greatest comfort level and the lowest possible risk to the mother and baby.

For most birthing options, including home births, you won't need to worry about gathering supplies for the delivery. However, for some birthing options, you and your partner may need to bring along clothes or personal hygiene items for an extended stay.

- **Hospital birthing rooms.** The most common place for delivery is still the hospital birthing room. In the movies, birthing rooms look scary: stainless steel lamps, cold tile floors, and a sterile operating room atmosphere. In real life, you might mistake a birthing room for a room at the Holiday Inn. They're comfortable, carpeted, and usually furnished with a couch, television, and private bathroom.

- **Home births.** About 5 percent of the time in the United States, mothers deliver in the comfort of their own home with the assistance of a midwife or physician. Many couples prefer that their children be born at home among family and friends rather than in a hospital among strangers.

  If you choose to deliver at home, be sure to have a backup physician in case unexpected complications arise. Home births are usually recommended only for women with low-risk pregnancies.
- **Birthing centers.** Birthing centers offer labor and delivery services, but rely on midwives to provide the majority of the patient care. Just as you would for home delivery, be sure to choose a backup physician in case of complications. The use of birthing centers is recommended for low-risk pregnancies only.
- **Other options.** Birthing chairs, Leboyer method births (quiet, more passive births with soft lights), and underwater deliveries are chosen by many couples. If you plan to utilize any of these alternatives, your preparations may be different from those for other birthing methods.

Little Worries

FATHERS-TO-BE tend to worry in the final stages of pregnancy. Most of the fears that erupt during this time stem from their lack of control over the event. Not knowing when she'll go into labor, whether she'll be able to reach you at work, or whether you can get her to the birthing place on time can cause great anxiety. Not knowing how much you can help during delivery or how much pain she will go through are just a few more of the great unknowns.

Here are the two biggest worries that fathers have and what you can do about them.

- **Worry #1. You won't get her to the hospital on time.**
  What if you take too long to get ready, or you hit traffic on the way to the hospital? No one wants his or her child born in the front seat of the family car on Route 11.

If you have this fear, relax. It would be extremely rare if your partner's water broke and she delivered her baby eight minutes later in the front hallway. I'm sure she wishes this type of thing were more common, but the odds are high that once you get to the birthing location and settle in, you will still have several hours to wait. For a first birth, the first stage of labor, characterized by contractions that occur from fifteen to twenty minutes apart, often lasts between ten and sixteen hours.

If you're still worried about your partner being one of the eight-minute wonders, drive the route to the birthing place several weeks before her due date to find the fastest and safest way to get there. Drive at different times of the day to experience traffic and road conditions. Approach the destination from your mother's house, the supermarket, and the shopping center.

Keep the gas tank full, the oil changed, the tires properly inflated—anything that will make you more comfortable about your ability to get her safely to the hospital on time. Pack your bags and keep them by the door. Have the phone number of a back up driver, a family member or friend, and a cab company nearby. That way, if she can't wait, another driver will be readily available. If you're planning a home birth, make sure the midwife's or doctor's number is handy, so she can call him or her before she calls you.

Drive at a safe speed. You will get there in plenty of time without having to use that red button under the dash that the dealer told you never to press unless faced with an extreme emergency involving interstate police.

- **Worry #2. You'll be at work when labor begins. She won't be able to reach you, or you won't get home in time.**
  If you are difficult to reach at work, or if you travel, consider renting a pager and/or cellular phone. Many hospitals have short-term contracts that allow you to rent the equipment on a monthly basis.

  If you are going to rely on a pager or cell phone, test it first. Have your partner call you so that both of you are familiar with any particular codes that must be used. Find out how long it takes before you get the message and can respond. Make sure the signal reaches you everywhere you go.

To cover all the bases, choose a backup person—a neighbor or family member—who can rush to your partner's aid, if need be. Designate a contact person at work who will make it his or her business to find you quickly.

The Worry Worksheet

ASIDE FROM THE TWO most common fears—not making it to the hospital on time and being unavailable when your partner needs you—there are plenty of other worries that may keep you awake at night. The best way to attack these fears is to identify them, then come up with a plan to handle them.

List your worries, keeping them as realistic as you can. Anxiety over whether you'll be a good delivery coach is one thing, but worrying about a meteor hitting the car on the way to the hospital is another. As you list your fears, write down what you can do to reduce the chance that they will happen.

I'm worried that_____

Here's what I can do to stop worrying so much or to reduce the chance that this will happen:

1. _____
2. _____
3. _____
4. _____
5. _____
6. _____
7. _____
8. _____
9. _____
10. _____

Pick two or three of these ideas and put them into action. This will help alleviate your concern, allowing you to move on.

Pssst—Beware of the Moon

Although there is no scientific evidence to back it up, many people who work in delivery rooms claim to see an increase in deliveries when the moon is full. It can't hurt to check the calendar for the closest full moon to your partner's due date. Put yourself on ultra yellow alert on that day.

Preparation List

IN THE LAST THREE months of pregnancy, you may notice your partner engaging in nesting activities. This refers to things she does to prepare for the baby's arrival. Baking, setting up the nursery, and stockpiling baby supplies are a few common activities. And, of course, she had her bag packed six weeks ago, ready to depart for the hospital.

Now, because fathers-to-be don't have an eight-pound reminder inside, kicking out in code, "Get ready because I'm coming soon," it's easy for us to put off these kinds of preparations. We tend to wait until our partner screams, "It's time! I think it's time!" before we look for the car keys or our glasses, or before we remember that we forgot to call the benefits office.

Take a hint from your partner. About a month or so before your baby arrives, start father nesting. Keep your hands busy and your mind occupied so that you don't have so much time to worry. Complete the following tasks, checking them off as you go.

- **You and your partner should request vacations or leaves of absence from your places of employment.** Complete any forms that may be required for advance approval.
- **Contact your benefits or insurance providers to find out what costs will be covered for the mother and child during labor, delivery, and recovery.** Some plans require prenotification during the pregnancy, as well as after the birth. You also may have to register the child within a month of the birth if you expect them to cover well-baby and other doctor appointments.
- **If your partner wants a private room, television, or daily newspaper during her hospital stay, contact the hospital to arrange for these services.**

- **Choose a name for the baby.** Although most couples have one or more names in mind, some wait until they see the baby to decide. The delay can cause arguments at the hospital, especially if the mother finds out that you've hated the names "Poindexter" and "Fanny" all along, but didn't want to say so. Men and women choose their children's names differently. Women tend to choose a name that holds a personal or family significance. Men choose a name that won't get the child beaten up in fourth grade. If at all possible, decide on a name in advance.
- **Choose a pediatrician.** It's smart to select your child's doctor with the same vigor you would use to chose a corporate officer for your company. After all, this individual will care for your greatest asset; you have the right to be choosy. In addition, check out the doctor's practice. What are the billing policies and office hours? Who are the doctor's partners? Would other doctors be on call in case of an emergency? If so, make sure you have the same confidence in them as you do in the primary physician.

Arranging for a Home Birth

A HOME BIRTH REQUIRES special preparations. In the last month of the pregnancy, you'll want to:

1. Choose a midwife or physician to deliver the baby.
2. Make sure the midwife or physician will be available around the clock.
3. Post the number of your midwife or physician near the phone.
4. Check with your insurance carriers for any additional forms that may be needed for a home birth.
5. Set up a room for the delivery, complete with a cassette player, relaxing tapes, books, and a phone.
6. Find out if the midwife or physician requires you to provide any supplies for the delivery.
7. Pack your father's bag.

If mothers can pack a bag for the hospital, so can fathers. Even if you plan a home delivery, it's still a good idea to gather everything you think you'll need. That way, you won't be tearing up the house, trying to find everything at the last minute.

Here's what your father's bag should include:

- **Books and magazines.** Remember, you may wait between ten and sixteen hours before the blessed event occurs. You might want something to read while your partner is resting.
- **Money.** It's a good idea to bring cash for coffee, snack machines, and the cafeteria. Bring change for making phone calls.
- **Tennis ball.** Some mothers-to-be have back pain during labor. A tennis ball rubbed against her back will often break up the spasms. You'll earn big points for this one.
- **Tape or disk player, tapes or CDs, and extra batteries.** Music will help both of you relax.
- **Comfortable clothes.** You'll be there awhile and may want to change, especially if you came to the hospital in the middle of the night or straight from work.
- **Contact lenses, glasses.** You may need to take your contacts out and put your glasses on. Don't forget the contact lens case and solutions.
- **Shaving kit.** Many hospital birthing rooms have shower facilities. You may want to clean up before the final stage of labor begins. A word of warning: Don't wait too long to take a shower. If you're soaping up when she's bearing down in the delivery room, you'll miss everything. Besides, you'll never live it down.
- **Snacks.** Choose nonperishable, energy-enhancing treats, such as trail mix.
- **A watch.** Most birthing rooms have wall clocks, but it's best to have either a digital watch or one with a second hand to time the contractions.
- **Insurance cards and forms.** Keep these at the top of the bag or in a side pocket. You'll need them when you check in.
- **Phone numbers.** List all the friends and family members who will want to know when the baby is born.
- **A camera/camcorder.** Don't leave home without one of these.
- **Focal point.** If you and your partner have practiced Lamaze breathing and relaxation, bring a favorite item to focus on.

And if you really want to fill that bag, bring:

- **The parts that were left over after you put together the crib, the bassinet, the playpen, the car seat, and the changing table.** Try to make a ham radio or time machine out of them. This will help you kill time (and relive those relaxed hours you spent inserting slotted bolt 1A into adjoining plastic mold 3G).
- **A pen, paper, and the names and addresses of the people who wrote the assembly instructions for the crib, the bassinet, the playpen, the car seat, and the changing table.** Express your true emotions about their easy-to-assemble products.

The Five Nicest Things You Can Do for the Mother-to-Be

IT'S IMPOSSIBLE TO fully appreciate what the mother experiences before, during, and after delivery. We can't begin to understand the physical, mental, hormonal, and emotional changes that she faces, but we can be supportive, caring, and understanding, especially during that long eighth month.

Need ideas? Use these tried-and-true methods:

- **Rub her feet.** Pregnant women carry so much additional weight that they almost always have sore feet.
- **Rub her neck, back, and shoulders.** Carrying the baby causes your partner to lean forward, which is hard on the muscles.
- **Support her by actions as well as words.** Show her that both of you are in this together. If she must give up caffeine, alcohol, or nicotine, you can do the same. Eat the same diet she eats, and when she exercises, work out with her.
- **Spend some quiet time together, doing things that both of you can do.** She may feel left out if you go rollerblading. Instead, rent a movie and spend a quiet evening together.
- **Help her deal with her own worries.** The worry worksheet you filled out earlier in this chapter works for moms, too.
- **Plan a short trip together.** Once the baby arrives, the two of you may get lost in the crowd. A month or two before the baby is due, take a short trip together. It'll do wonders for the spirit.

Crib Notes

Tip #1. Get a private room.

If at all possible, get a private room at the hospital or birthing center. It's usually not much more expensive than a regular room, and it's worth every penny to ensure your partner a little more sleep and privacy. Also, it's easier for family and friends to visit when there is only one person in the room. Some private rooms feature small refrigerators, better views, and gourmet meals.

Tip #2. Make a time capsule.

Many fathers create a time capsule when their children are born. Gather pictures, newspapers from the day your child was born, a letter from you, and anything else you can think of. Put these in a safe place and give them to your child when he or she is old enough to appreciate them.

Resources

Books

Eisenberg, Arlene, Heidi E. Murkoff, and Sandee E. Hathaway. *What to Expect When You're Expecting.* New York: Workman Publishing, 1984.

Fournier, Barbara, and George Fournier. *Pre-Parenting, A Guide for Planning Ahead.* New Jersey: Prentice-Hall, 1980.

Kitzinger, Sheila. *Homebirth: The Essential Guide to Giving Birth Outside of the Hospital.* New York: Dorling Kindersley, 1991.

Williams, Gene B. *The New Father's Panic Book: Everything a Dad Needs to Know to Welcome His Bundle of Joy.* New York: Avon Books, 1997.

Organizations

Auto Safety Hotline
1-800-424-9393

Informed Homebirth
P.O. Box 3675
Ann Arbor, MI 48106
(313) 662-6857

NEW PARENTS AND BABIES 101

Why is it that all babies look like Winston Churchill?
—Everett De Morier (before he had kids)

I remember vividly when Debbie was pregnant with Nick and we saw the first real ultrasound, where the baby actually resembled something other than a sea monkey. To this day, I remember looking at that screen, seeing his profile, watching him move, knowing that, in a few months, I would be the proud father of—Elvis. Our child looked like Elvis Presley, with the forming head making a perfect pompadour. The name stuck. Cards, letters, and phone calls came in from family and friends, all wanting to know how Little Elvis was doing.

And then the day came. After several hours of hard labor, Elvis had wiggled down as far as someone of his stature and girth could, then he called for a cab to take him the rest of the way. The hospital set up for a Cesarean section, and, minutes later, he was born. Once I saw him more clearly, he didn't look like Elvis at all. He looked more like The Michelin Man.

Women and Labor

MOST NEW FATHERS are surprised by the carnival atmosphere surrounding birth. They expect this to be a private moment between the mother, the father, the baby, and the doctor. In reality, during the three stages of labor, doctors, nurses, medical students, interns, anesthesiologists, the guy who cleans the carpets, and Crazy Zimo from the car wash next door may be going in and out of the room. Porn stars have fewer people see them naked than a woman in labor. Yet, whenever I've asked a mother about this, she has said that, during the final stages of labor, she would not have cared if the U.S. Marine Band was in the room. For many first-time fathers, this can be an uncomfortable realization.

Remember that the new mother has a lot on her mind. She is facing hormonal changes, physical changes, recovery from delivery (and possibly from surgery), mental and emotional stress, and, most likely, the greatest weight loss and fitness recovery plan of her life. Under the circumstances, a little public nudity might seem like the least of her worries.

Four Ways to Help Mom through the First Month

- **Create mini mom-vacations.** We still do this one. Debbie's mother goes out of town frequently, so once a month I send Debbie to her mother's for a Friday night getaway. She relaxes, reads, takes a bath, sleeps in, and soaks up all the silence. She comes home rested and relaxed, and I get to leave the toilet seat up, drink from the milk carton, rent *Amazon Women from the Avocado Jungle of Death,* and be a slob until the next morning. Then I frantically put the house back together and pretend it was like that all along.

  Day trips are often just as relaxing as overnight ones. Once or twice a month, help the new mom think of something she'd like to do for the day. Get her friends and family involved; plan a girls night out, a shopping trip, lunches, or time at the movies.
- **Pamper her.** I could not help feeling an incredible amount of respect for Debbie as I watched her during the birth process. If

it had been me lying there, I would have demanded an epidural and a divorce after my first Braxton Hicks (painless preparatory contractions).

After nine months of carrying a child and going through the most incredible pain of her life, the new mother deserves a little pampering. Buy a gift certificate so that she can get a massage or have a facial—anything to allow her to be coddled and fawned over for a few hours.

- **Support her fitness and weight loss plan.** It's very easy to say, "Good luck at the gym. Oh, and on your way home, could you pick up some pork rinds and a twelve-pack?" It's an entirely different thing to work alongside her as she sets out to achieve her fitness and weight loss goals. It takes between one and two months for a woman's pelvic floor—the muscles that support her bowels, bladder, and womb—to regain their strength. With daily exercise, it may take three months or longer before her figure returns to normal.
- **Give sleep, the gift that keeps on giving.** Even though you may have gone back to work a week or two after the baby was born, take your turn with bottle feeding and diaper changing. To help the new mother regain her strength, make sure she gets plenty of rest.

The Baby Blues and Postpartum Depression

BETWEEN 50 AND 75 PERCENT of all new mothers suffer from the baby blues. It usually begins a day or two after delivery, and can lead to weepiness, irritability, impatience, restlessness, and anxiety. Symptoms usually disappear on their own within a few days, often as quickly as they came.

Postpartum depression, which is more serious, affects about one in ten new mothers. It usually starts a week or two after the baby is born and leaves the mother feeling weepy, irritable, confused, sluggish, tired, and hopeless. Symptoms can range from mild to severe. If they persist more than a few weeks, contact your doctor.

Hormonal changes have been blamed for both the baby blues and postpartum depression. In addition to these biological reasons, the new mother has emotional justification for feeling anxious and uncertain. Once the father goes back to work and family and friends don't stop by as often, she may feel overwhelmed by the responsibility of being the primary caretaker for an infant. She may also experience a form of attention withdrawal after missing the attention she received at the hospital.

Quick Treatments for the
Baby Blues and Postpartum Depression

1. **Create time.** Ask the new mother whether she needs alone time, couple time, or friend time. Give her what she needs.

2. **Make sure she eats well.** A good diet and mild exercise are the best treatments. They'll also take her mind off her daily frustrations. Carbohydrates will provide a good, steady supply of energy, and protein is important, too. Whole wheat cereals, yogurt or eggs, fruit, whole grain breads, healthy sandwiches, and rice and pasta dishes should be on the menu. Alcohol, caffeine, and nicotine should be avoided during this time.

3. **Help her find other new mothers who have also suffered from the baby blues or postpartum depression.** Ask your doctor if there is a new-mothers group in your area. Find a new-mothers chat room on the Internet. Just knowing she isn't the only one who has ever suffered from the baby blues or postpartum depression can be very comforting.

4. **Accept offers of help from friends, neighbors, and family.** The new mom may smile and say that she'll be fine while you're at work, but will she? At least for the first three or four weeks, try to recruit as much help as you possibly can to share the housework, prepare meals, or just visit.

5. **Make sleep a priority.** Help her get as much sleep as possible. Most newborns sleep about eighteen hours a day. Encourage her to sleep whenever the baby does.

6. **Get someone to help with the housework.** Who needs this burden on top of everything else? When someone wants an idea for a baby gift, suggest that a cleaning service for the first two months would be a fantastic present.

7. Get her out of the house periodically. Every now and then, the new mom needs a break from the baby. Ask friends and relatives to baby-sit for short periods so she can get away.

8. Help her stay in touch with friends. With all the changes that are occurring, the new mom needs a little stability and friendship. An hour spent talking to a friend at a local restaurant can be a real pick-me-up.

9. Accept imperfection. Everything is not going to go as planned. Your partner might need to adjust her expectations, just as you may need to adjust yours.

New Father Postpartum

MOTHERS AREN'T THE only ones who are affected by the baby blues. Many fathers complain of mild depression, uneasiness, and feelings of helplessness. Studies show that most new fathers are unlikely to have these emotions at the same time as their partners; for some reason, the father's feelings of sadness often increase when the new mother is feeling great.

Most of us muddle through, feeling silly and a little guilty that we are sad. That's not going to help. First of all, realize that it's both normal and temporary. Then, identify the strongest emotion you are feeling. Are you more stressed out than anything? More confined? More confused? From that, you can figure out a cure. Maybe you need some alone time, some friend time, or some quiet time. Maybe you need to go to a movie or spend an hour in a crowded sports bar, screaming at a television screen. Maybe you need to sit near a stream with a fishing pole.

Whatever you do, don't feel guilty. Taking a few hours for yourself is as important as giving that time to your partner, because if you're not on top of your game, you won't be as helpful or as supportive as you want to be.

Gaining Your Father Confidence

I REMEMBER WHEN Nick was born and we needed to change him for the first time. Debbie and I looked at each other as if we'd just been asked to take out Mrs. Pelson's gallbladder, but we gamely gave it a try.

I wish I had videotaped it, because it was more like a mugging than anything else. We two adults tried to corner this wiggling kid and find out what kind of credit cards he was carrying. When we'd finished, the diaper stayed on for about thirty seconds. In time, we learned to diaper with confidence. By two months, we could do any number of advanced diapering moves. We could diaper a baby while in a car or in a wind tunnel, while jogging, or—the most advanced maneuver of all—while mowing the lawn.

The confidence that you need will come very quickly. By two months, there will be few baby maintenance jobs you haven't yet mastered. However, there will be certain things you will never feel confident doing. For instance, I would not even clip the toenails on our dog, much less the tiny fingernails of our children. I did not want to clip off the tip of a finger and have them miss a brilliant career as a concert pianist or safe cracker, all because of me. Let Debbie have that guilt.

Crying

MOST BABIES CRY for an average of two to three hours a day for the first seven weeks. The length of time that a newborn cries tends to peak at around three hours a day when they are six weeks old. It slowly decreases to an hour or two by twelve weeks.

Types of Newborn Cries

The soft, cooing cry. This cry is heard within the first twenty minutes of birth and on many television commercials, and is never heard again. Don't get used to this one.

The "come and feed me" cry. This one is very straightforward, often occurring around scheduled feeding times. It's a potent, frequent reminder of the baby's incredible powers, should he or she ever decide to use them for evil.

The "drop what you're doing" cry. This is the fire whistle of cries. Its message is clear: "I don't care what you're doing or who you're talking to. Get in my office in twenty seconds, or there will be hell to pay, mister."

The "twenty questions" cry. This one is a loud, piercing cry, usually occurring between the hours of 1:00 A.M. and 3:00 A.M. Half the fun is guessing what caused the cry and how to stop it. You'll find yourself asking, "What? Are you hungry? Do you need to be changed? Rocked? Burped? Walked, coddled, talked to, tutored? What is it? Please tell me!! What!?!?"

The "Trumpets of Babylon" cry. This is the one where you can identify at least three voices in one: the eerie baby cry. It's a good idea to keep holy water nearby, just in case things get out of hand.

The ear bleeder. This cry will find C3 on your spinal column and root around in there with a rusty knife. It has been known to interfere with satellite transmissions and open electric garage doors. Intense listening to this cry has been linked to permanent brain damage in laboratory rats.

The "why didn't I choose parents who could take care of me properly?" cry. This is the inconsolable cry of a colicky baby.

When a Newborn Won't Stop Crying

- **Try a rocking chair.** Babies are often soothed by the motion.
- **Put the baby in the stroller and go for a walk.** I spent hours pushing Nick in the stroller between rooms.
- **Go for a ride in the car.** The car often has a magical effect on babies. Many parents tell tales of 3:00 A.M. rides to stop the neighbors from calling the authorities. The problem is, the baby often wakes up when you're trying to get him or her out of the car seat and into the crib. The best thing to do is use a baby seat with a carrier that comes away from the base. Then, when you stop the car, simply leave the baby in the carrier, detach it from the base, and put the carrier, baby and all, into the crib. Nick spent the first four months of his life sleeping in such a way.
- **Lay the baby across your knees and rub his or her back.** Besides soothing the baby, this can release stubborn gas bubbles, which is often the problem.
- **Try a music box or mobile.** Babies hear just like we do, only they can't make sense of the sounds. Often, a methodical rhythm or soft beat takes them back to the womb and helps them relax.

- **Give the baby a bath.** Sometimes, warm water and fresh clothes will soothe a newborn.
- **Make a sound, any sound.** Many babies are soothed by a low hum or the sound of a running dryer, vacuum cleaner, air conditioner, or blender. You can buy CDs and cassettes of these sounds for the baby's room, or you can make them yourself. If you choose the dryer method, never leave the baby sitting on top of it in an infant seat, unattended.
- **When all else fails, let the baby scream.** If you've checked out every option—food, diapers, and gas being the big three—and you can't think of anything else, it's far better to walk away and let the baby cry for a few minutes than to risk permanent nerve damage. Place the baby in a safe place, such as a playpen or crib, walk out of the room, take deep cleansing breaths, and after a safe interval, go back in.

The Great Pacifier Debate

Believe it or not, this is a big issue in the world of child care. Some experts even use the term "pacifier dependent," alluding to strung-out newborns who hock their mother's jewelry, just to get a fix.

Like most parents, Debbie and I had decided that we were not going to use a pacifier with Nick. Exactly forty-eight hours after we brought him home, Nick was corked up with a Winnie the Pooh pacifier, and I was having more flown in daily. (To see what the big deal was, I tried one of Nick's pacifiers myself. I liked his cat rattle better.)

There's one big problem with giving children pacifiers: they get used to an outside source of relaxation. Parents may have to stumble into their children's room in the middle of the night to give them the pacifier because they can't get it for themselves. There are also issues involving teeth and the damage that a pacifier can do.

My philosophy is that during the first year, who cares? Nick used pacifiers at night until he was two-and-a-half. Then Santa came and took them for all the new babies at the hospital who needed them. We went through months of preparation. We explained that Santa needed these pacifiers and the babies were counting on them. We promised that Santa would leave a toy in place of them. We prepared ourselves to deal with his withdrawal. When it actually happened, Nick just said, "Cool. Whatever," and played with the bounty Mr. Claus had brought him.

Get used to it. There are things you'll say you are going to do when you're parents, and there are things you'll actually do. We said we'd never give our kids a pacifier, we'd never have the television on at the dinner table, we'd never bribe our kids with dessert to eat dinner—the list goes on and on. Ever so slowly, items like these get scribbled off the list to make room for what's really important. Don't beat yourself up if your ideas about childrearing change after birth. You're just taking information from the field and making adjustments as you go.

Mailing Lists

WHEN YOUR CHILD is born, you will be added to half a quazillion mailing lists. Soon your mailbox will be filled with information on everything from life insurance to educational toys, and salespeople will call you trying to sell those same products. It can be tough to resist, because these companies sell safety, enrichment, or education for your child.

"... and you do want a happy and healthy child don't you, sir?"

"Sure."

"Of course you do. So I just need to confirm a few things to get you going. Do you still live on Mayberry Avenue?"

"Yeah."

Wham. You've just signed up for the Endangered Species of the Month Video Collection. Be careful.

Crib Notes

Tip #3. *Buy a swing that winds silently.*

If your child is soothed by the rocking of the swing and you have to rewind it when it slows down, the POCKITA-POCKITA sound of a swing without the silent-wind feature will surely send the baby through the roof. Also, get a swing that offers easy entry, with a front that opens like a door. Children are more likely to remain asleep if you take them out through the easy entry door than if you hit their head taking them out through the top.

Tip #4. *Buy black and white stuff.*

Newborns can only see about eight to fourteen inches from their face, and they cannot see colors clearly. However, they love black and white objects. A few years ago, some clever merchandisers realized this and started producing black and white stuffed animals, posters, and toys. When Nick was born, a friend told us about the best of these: black and white plastic rings that hook together and look a little like shower-curtain holders. They are worth their weight in formula. You can hook them to the baby swing, the crib, the bassinet, or the car seat. Even at the earliest stages of infancy, a child will remain focused on them because of the contrast in light and dark. As they grow, they'll reach for them and play with them.

Tip #5. *Try to take the baby outside every day.*

Most doctors agree that there is no reason why a healthy baby under a year old shouldn't be taken outside for a few minutes every day. Cold weather is not dangerous to a newborn, as long as his or her skin is protected.

Resources

Books

Brazelton, T. Berry. *Touchpoints, The Essential Reference: Your Child's Emotional and Behavioral Development*. New York: Addison-Wesley Publishing Company, 1994.

Eisenberg, Arlene, Heidi E. Murkoff, and Sandee E. Hathaway. *What to Expect the First Year.* New York: Workman Publishing, 1989.

Fairview Health Service. *Caring for You and Your Baby: From Pregnancy through the First Year of Life*. Minneapolis: Fairview Press, 1997.

Leach, Penelope. *Your Baby and Child: From Birth to Age Five*. New York: Alfred A. Knopf, 1997.

Stoutt, Glenn R. Jr. *The First Month of Life: A Parents Guide to Care of a Newborn*. Oradell, New Jersey: Medical Economics Company, Book Division, 1977.

Junk Mail

You can be taken off both mail and phone solicitation lists by writing to either source below. State that you want your name taken off any current or future lists. Note: This will not stop those people who call after seeing the newspaper birth announcements.

Mail Preference Service
Direct Marketing Association
P.O. Box 9008
Farmingdale, NY 11738-9008

Director of List Maintenance
ADVO
239 W. Service Road
Hartford, CT 06120-1280

Other Resources

The American Academy of Pediatrics
P.O. Box 927
Elks Grove Village, IL 60009-0927
Send a self-addressed, stamped envelope for a free *Parents' Resource Guide.*

America Online has a great site called *Moms Online.* This source has everything from chat rooms to support groups to general information for parents, and contains information on mothers' groups in your area. Go to keyword: *Moms Online.*

EIGHT POUNDS, TWELVE OUNCES

James: *"Well you don't look so hot yourself, you know."*
Mollie: *"Why don't you try squeezing something the size of a watermel-on out an opening the size of a lemon, and you see how hot you look."*
James: *"Ouch. I should call my mother more often."*

—Look Who's Talking

A h, the first month of fatherhood! A time when we buy a box of cigars for our friends at work, who inevitably toss them into a desk drawer and forget about them until retirement. A time when we discover how to feed a baby and operate the remote control at the same time. A time when we subscribe to the Toy of the Month Club at only twelve easy payments of $29 each. A time when we've captured three-quarters of the life of a month-old baby on videotape.

The first month of fatherhood fits somewhere between being a newlywed and being a bona fide dad. You're still pumped with adrenaline after the excitement of the birth. People are still stopping by to see the new baby and dropping off gifts. As congratulation cards and calls continue to pour in, your mother-in-law stops by with those wonderful tuna and bologna casseroles, your brother-in-law mows the lawn, and Mrs. Carmichael from church brings a pie to the house. Although you may go through periods of sleep deprivation and con-fusion—and even though you often search frantically for a work shirt with no baby vomit on it—the scent of new baby is still in the air.

Of course each father's reaction is different, just as each baby is different. Our first son, Nick, was a high-maintenance, colicky fireball. He wanted to eat, cry, eat, poop, complain, cry, cry, and if he had time and there was nothing on TV, he'd cry. He scheduled quick pockets of sleep for times when it was impossible for anyone else to nap, and we were convinced he was mentioned in Revelations by name. Week by week, he became a happier baby; he finally slept through the night at ten weeks.

Alex, our second child, was completely different. He wanted to eat and sleep in the baby swing. That's it. I'd try to hold him and walk with him, and he'd give me a look that said, "Just put me in the swing."

Being the intelligent, caring parent that I was, I'd hold him or rock him or talk to him, and once again, he would look up, as if to say, "Look, it's simple. You put me in the swing; I stop crying. Now just put me in there, wind me up, and go away!" When I didn't respond, he'd get frustrated and start to fuss. "You either put me in the swing, and I will stare at the wall, coo, and then go to sleep, or don't put me in the swing, and I will retch and scream and cry until I've created a hell for you unlike anything you've ever experienced. What'll it be?"

So I put Alex in the swing, he tipped me five bucks, and we've gotten along great ever since.

The First Month Checklist

DURING THE FIRST month, new fathers are a little tired, a little excited, a little worried, and a little numb, sometimes all at the same time. It's a back-slapping, picture-carrying, coffee-chugging, spit-up-cleaning, camcorder-using, diaper-changing, belly-button-cleaning time.

Here's where all the preparations you've made will pay off. Your baby may sleep first in a bassinet or crib in your room, and later be moved into a separate room. There, you will already have stashed sleepers and clothes in generic colors, as well as diapers, baby lotion, burp cloths, bottles, bibs, and formula.

Your days will look like this: four hours feeding the baby, three hours soothing the baby, four hours doing baby laundry, three hours changing diapers, six hours walking with the baby, three hours doing more baby laundry, and four hours sleeping. This adds up to twenty-seven hours. Stop sleeping, and you'll have an hour to spare.

Some Other Things to Do

1. Place the new baby on a benefit package. Many benefit packages require you to call your insurance carrier within a few days of the child's birth.

2. Create a schedule. Come up with a rough schedule for the first month. Write down everything that needs to be done, including errands, grocery shopping, bills that need to be paid, and housecleaning. This is really more of a list than a schedule, because the baby will pretty much determine the when and where of everything for awhile.

3. Send out the birth announcements and thank-you cards. Proper etiquette says you should get these out within the first month. If there are many to respond to, you and your partner can do a few each night.

4. Adjust your work schedule. Take a look at the next four weeks, as far as work is concerned. What's coming up? What needs more of your attention? Is it possible to work from home for a while?

5. Plan to take on the majority of the housework, or hire someone to come in. Look at what needs to be done around the house and create a plan to take care of it, along with your other responsibilities. A cleaning service that comes in once or twice a week is relatively inexpensive, and would make a great gift from someone.

6. Arrange for some help for your partner. If needed, arrange for a nurse or someone to help with the baby after you go back to work. Many qualified people offer home aid to people recovering from surgery. Many of these individuals will clean, make meals, and do whatever else it is that you need.

7. Arrange meals. If you're not the cook in the house and don't plan on eating pizza for a month, you'll need to arrange meals. Take advantage of family and neighbors when they ask if there is anything they can do. Ask them to bring over casseroles or cold cuts.

8. Consider a diaper service. For the first few months, this would be a wonderful gift to give yourself. You'll save on the cost of disposable diapers, as well as the time and energy required to maintain a diaper pail. You simply store the soiled diapers, and the service picks them up and brings you fresh replacements.

The Help Registry

ONE PHRASE YOU'LL hear often from neighbors and family is, "Let us know if there's anything you need." Most of the time, these offers are sincere. Make a list of all the little things that are difficult for you and your partner to do. Are you having trouble running errands, walking the dog, or preparing meals? Do you need groceries?

These are your neighbors, family, and friends. Take them up on their kind offer, and return the favor when you can.

Definitions

GLANCE OVER THIS SHORT collection of terms and refer to them as needed.

Apgar test. This is the first test that babies are given after birth. The child is tested for vital signs, including color, lung strength, and muscle flexibility. The scores from this test are recorded at one and five minutes after birth. A score of seven or better signifies good general health.

Babinski reflex. When the sole of the foot is stroked, the foot flares up and turns inward.

Brachial pulse. Pulse rate taken from the baby's upper arm. Normal range for infants is between 100 and 130 beats per minute when asleep, between 140 and 160 when awake, and 160 to 200 when crying.

Colic. Thought to be caused by gas, which leads to uncontrollable crying and discomfort.

Colostrum. The pre-milk that comes from a mother's breast and contains important antibodies that the baby's body cannot produce.

Combs test. Blood is taken from the baby's heel to screen for low blood sugar, sickle-cell anemia, and other conditions.

Cradle cap. An oily scalp, which is common in newborns.

Denver Developmental Screening Test. A test used to determine an infant's development. The test is given when a child fails to complete three tasks that 90 percent of other infants his or her age have achieved.

Croup. An inflammation of the respiratory passages that produces labored breathing, a sharp barking cough, and wheezing.

Epstein's pearls. Yellowish-white spots on the roof of a baby's mouth that disappear without treatment.

Fontanelle. The "soft spots" on the baby's head, which later close up with the formation of bone.

Icterus. Another name for jaundice.

Thrush. A fungus that produces milky-white patches on a baby's mouth, lips, and throat. Usually treated with an antifungal agent.

Useful Family Information

- Babies under one year of age can become violently ill by eating honey. Honey contains spores called *clostridium botulinum*—which can cause botulism in infants.
- Some sand that is used in sandboxes or under swing sets contains tremolite. This fiber floats in the air, gets caught in the lungs, and can cause health problems.
- The old saying, "A cat will steal a baby's breath," is not completely wrong. A small warm body that smells like milk can be very attractive to cats. This can be dangerous if the cat inhibits a child's breathing. Just to play it safe, put a mosquito net over the bassinet or crib, or close the door when the baby is sleeping.
- Feel the baby's forehead while you are burping him or her. If the forehead is cool, there is still a gas bubble that needs to be released.
- A bath in unscented Dove or Ivory soap will heal even the most stubborn diaper rash in three days.
- Mistletoe can be deadly if eaten by an infant. It's a good idea to keep it out of your house until the baby is older, and to make sure it isn't in homes where the child will be spending time.

Useless Family Information

- On the island of Lan Yu near Taiwan, if the wife does not have a baby, the husband is blamed, disgraced, and divorced.
- Seven thousand babies are born each year to fathers over the age of fifty-five.
- According to a *Women's World* study, full-time homemakers work 99.6 hours a week.
- Grown-ups outnumber kids three-and-a-half to one at Disneyland.

- A baby under six months of age breathes only through its nose.
- A newborn baby's body is only 20 percent of its adult size, but its brain is 90 percent.
- Generally, girls walk two weeks earlier than boys.
- Single men make up 13 percent of the population, but commit 90 percent of all violent crimes. (Debbie made me put that one in.)
- Girl babies smile more than boy babies do.
- A producing dairy cow is pregnant 75 percent of the time.
- Babies are born with 300 bones. Many of these fuse together; when children grow into adults, they have 206 bones.
- Four out of five left-handed children are born to right-handed parents.
- Mothers with three or more children tend to live longer than mothers with only one child.
- It takes a housefly sixty days to become a great-grandmother.
- Statistically speaking, babies born in May weigh more, have higher IQs, and live longer.
- A baby's face is an eighth of its head size; an adult's face is half of its head size.

The First Year Checklist

IT'S IRONIC. For almost a year, we wait for the arrival of the baby. We plan for the day our child is born, but not for the baby's first year, even though our lives will change in so many ways during that twelve-month period. By asking questions and preparing a rough plan for our first year as fathers, we can save ourselves time, money, and frustration.

Are you both going back to work full time?

This is a decision that is often made early in the pregnancy, but many couples change their minds as the last week of maternity/paternity leave draws closer.

In 1993, The Family and Medical Leave Act was passed. This covers workers who are employed by a company with more than fifty employees. The employee must have worked for at least twelve months, and must have accrued more than 1,250 hours working for that employer. Fathers and mothers who meet the criteria have the right to take an unpaid leave of absence for up to twelve weeks for the birth or adoption of a child.

If you have the money to take time off, you and/or your partner can spend those twelve weeks with the baby. It's a great time to see whether being a stay-at-home parent is a good fit.

If both of you are going back to work, how will you divide up the household tasks?

Go over each duty and decide who will do what, how, and when. Deciding this early before it becomes an issue will save you time and frustration.

What about daycare and baby-sitting?

Finding the right daycare provider can be as challenging as finding the right job or buying the right house. It's a crucial decision, because the person you choose will manage and protect your most precious charge. Even if you or your partner will be staying home with the baby, you'll still need a baby-sitter when you want to run to the gym. You'll also need a sitter when you and your partner want to slip out to a movie so you can smell air that isn't permeated with the scent of diaper wipes.

- **Try to identify at least two places where you can drop the baby off, and accumulate the names of people who can come over within an hour's notice.** These can be family members or friends, but don't wait until the last minute to find them. If your attempts to find time alone are frustrated too often, you may feel resentment toward the baby.
- **Create a baby-sitter fund.** Add to this fund every week and build it up so that paying the baby-sitter is never an issue if you or your partner need to get out to recharge your batteries.

Where to Find a Baby-Sitter?

1. Ask your friends and family. There is no better source than the people you know and trust.

2. Ask your neighbors. Having a baby-sitter close to home might give you a chance to see them in action before you hire them.

3. Call your church, synagogue, or community center.

4. Call the family education department at your local college. College students are often very reliable baby-sitters, and they can drive themselves.

5. Contact the County Office for Children or look in the phone book under "County Government." Often, these groups have lists of qualified baby-sitters and daycare providers.

Make Sure Your Baby-sitter Knows . . .

- **The location of the information sheet.** This is a list of phone numbers, including where you'll be, your cellular phone or pager number, and emergency phone numbers (fire, ambulance, police, poison control, the child's doctor, the closest neighbor or relative). It should also contain information about the child's allergies or medical needs.
- **Where the first-aid supplies are kept.**
- **The locations of all exits and entrances to the house.**
- **The locations of all fire escape routes.**
- **Where flashlights and candles are kept.**
- **Any security system shut-offs or code words.**
- **Your child's routine and the house rules.** You can help by telling the sitter about the child's favorite toy or activity. Tell him or her what and how much the child can eat or drink, how the child likes to sleep, where extra clothing is located, what habits your child has, and how to take care of the pets. Be sure to leave a consent form and information about your medical insurance coverage, in case your child needs to receive medical treatment.

What about religious concerns?

Will you have the child baptized, christened, or circumcised? If you both come from different religious backgrounds, what will the compromise be? Discuss this between yourselves as early as possible, and then discuss it with your families.

What will you do this holiday season?

Most likely, your families have traditions for the holidays. If you and your partner both have parents who have divorced and remarried, you may have four families that will want you and the baby to be there. Think about how you can accommodate as many needs as possible and create the best compromise.

Unless your name is Hatfield and your partner's is McCoy, why not bring all the families together? If the baby is very young, the best idea might be to host the holidays at your house. That way, you won't have to drag eighty pounds of baby equipment all over town, and you won't have to worry about forgetting something important. Use an open-house format so you're not buried with having to serve a sit-down dinner to thirty people.

What should you do with cash gifts for the baby?

Most likely, some well-wishers gave you small gifts of cash to welcome the new addition. Consider putting the money in a savings account. If you received more than $250, you could start a mutual fund. Depending on the fund, the money could grow at a much faster rate than in a savings account.

How much will you need to budget for the next year to cover birthdays, holidays, baby clothes, and medical bills not covered by insurance?

Calculate how much you think you'll need for the entire year for each item, then divide by twelve. Every month, put away that amount so you'll have the money you need.

Crib Notes

Tip #6. *Keep a cold air humidifier running.*

Babies can't blow their nose, and they need to keep their nasal passages moist. Keep a humidifier running, especially at night when your furnace is on.

Tip #7. *Plan meals ahead of time.*

Take out a cookbook and plan seven main dishes. These might include soups, stews, and casseroles. Buy the ingredients to make two of each main course. Double up on the cooking; in other words, as long as you're making one hamburger casserole, you might as well make two. Freeze one of the casseroles in meal-sized portions that you can reheat later. Freeze whatever you don't eat of the other casserole, too. If you think ahead, you can limit your grocery shopping to twice a month. You'll see the savings in time and money, and you'll always have a nutritious meal just a few minutes away.

Tip #8. *Establish visiting hours.*

By creating specific times for friends and family to visit, you will reduce drop-ins and give the mother more time to rest.

Resources

Books

Lees, Christoph, Karina Reynolds, and Grainne McCartan. *Pregnancy and Birth: Your Questions Answered.* New York: Dorling Kindersley, 1997.

Schmitt, Barton D. *Your Child's Health: The Parent's Guide to Symptoms, Emergencies, Common Illnesses, Behavior, and School Problems.* New York: Bantam Books, 1991.

Other Resources

U.S. Department of Labor
Employment Standards Administration
Wage and Hour Division
Washington, DC. 20210
Write for more information on The Family and Medical Leave Act.

✒ CAPTAIN'S LOG ✐

Some people never go crazy.
What truly horrible lives they must lead.
—Barfly

Comedian Bill Cosby believes you're not a parent until you have two kids, because until then, if something is broken, you know who did it.

My version is this: you're not a parent until people stop dropping by with tuna noodle casseroles, bath thermometers shaped like ducks, and sleepers with Mickey Mouse on them. Once that day comes, you begin to travel the road of fatherhood.

Losing sleep and taking care of a recuperating wife are just the beginning. When Alex was a baby, I was impressed with how alert I was, even though I only slept for three or four hours each night. Then one day, I warmed up a bottle and handed it to Alex and put the bib around Debbie's neck. She gave me that look, the one that says, "How can I have your genes removed from these children?"

Just as I thought I couldn't go on without getting more sleep, Alex began sleeping through the night. I awoke from my first night's sleep in weeks, ran to the nursery in a complete panic, knocking things over as I went, fearing that I had left him in the car by mistake. All of my racket woke him up and eliminated any hope that he would fall asleep again.

By the time the baby is two or three months old, the initial excitement has begun to fade. You've taken the six-foot stork back to the rental place, have probably gone back to work, and are now trying to squeeze all the tasks of your pre-baby life into the smaller slices of time and energy that are now available.

Sleep

REGARDLESS OF WHETHER you're up at night feeding the baby or awake because the baby has cried and your wife is nursing, you're probably not getting a solid night's sleep during the first month of your child's life. The good news is that almost half of all babies sleep through the night by two months, and over three-quarters do so by three months. So the odds are in your favor that you'll be enjoying a normal night's rest in about eight weeks.

Change

NOW THAT'S A NASTY word—change. How we receive and use change, how we accept and enjoy it and react to the child's first month of life, is different for every father. The way we deal with change varies even with the birth of each child.

For example, I was more relaxed after Alex, our second, was born. I knew the basics. I had read through the labor and delivery script, and even played the part once in an off-Broadway production, to some very promising reviews. I knew how labor would go. Debbie would rest, go through mild discomfort, then descend into brain-melting labor pain. I even knew that when the pain was at its worst, she'd grit her teeth, curse my ancestors to eternal damnation, and tell the labor nurse that I had cheated on my driving test. And then, the baby would come, and she'd say, "I don't want ANY more kids," just as she had after Nick was born.

While promoting *Crib Notes for the First Year of Marriage: A Survival Guide for Newlyweds,* I was often asked for the most important piece of advice I could give to newly married couples. My answer? That the first year of marriage is a time of great change, even if the man and woman have known each other for some time, lived together, and already solved the problem about the toilet seat. Sure, they expect some change, but when there is more change than they had anticipated, they're confused and surprised. So my main message to new couples was this: expect change, use it, and learn from it.

For new fathers, the exact same message applies. We know that we won't be able to be on four softball teams anymore, or that we can't have poker night at our place every Tuesday because it will interfere with the baby's sleep schedule, or that money may be tight for a while. But almost all fathers seem surprised when these changes and others actually occur.

Now, so far, this doesn't sound like fun. You may think that you have cursed yourself to a lifetime of lugging diaper bags, wearing Bermuda shorts, and carrying car seats. In other words, you've taken on a life of drudgery: a life where your only choice is to sell the Corvette, buy a minivan, and learn to love Yahtzee.

Not true.

As humans, our tendency is to resist any kind of change. But change is the way we move to the next level of development.

There is a very famous *New Yorker* cover entitled "A New Yorker's View of the World." In the foreground, there's a rooftop view of Fifth Avenue in detail; a block away, Seventh Avenue is a little smaller; Forty-Third Street is smaller yet; and beyond that, another block away, there's Africa.

This is how you'll look back at your child's first year. You'll remember bringing the baby home, noticing when the umbilical cord fell off, giving the child his or her first bath—and then, suddenly, before you know it, the child will have conned you into giving him or her an illegal cookie at 7:00 A.M.

It's true that, during the second and third month, Captain Reality comes to visit. Sometimes in that first month, we fear we'll don a dress and climb a water tower with a deer rifle. Then, something changes. We can just make out the shores of Africa in the distance. Our memory of the difficult time fades, and we look forward to that first smile, first laugh, first crawl, first step, and first word.

What happens during the first months of fatherhood is different for everyone. Some men fit every slice of their existing lives into the new lifestyle without much trouble. Others, like me, try to squeeze that old schedule, that old routine, into a smaller box. I still wanted to work out three times a week, mountain bike on Saturdays, work late, go golfing, and play on the Internet until 4:00 A.M. Maybe you have the same expectations.

That's not to say that you can never do these things again. But you may have to work out in the mornings now, or during lunch. Maybe you'll have to take work home, or work at home a few days a week, or get to the office earlier. Maybe you'll have to combine a golf outing with a business lunch. Or, maybe you'll have to accept the fact that you can't do it all.

Remember that the definition of insanity is using the same process and expecting different results. It goes like this: we starve ourselves, work out every day for a month to lose twelve pounds, and then gain it back. A few months later, we have a great idea: we'll starve ourselves, work out every day, lose the same twelve pounds, and gain it back. A few months later, we do it all over again.

When we fail to achieve a goal, it often means that our system has failed. Once we realize that we've been using a method that doesn't work, we should simply file this information away and try a different method. Each time we do, we're closer to finding a system that will work for us. Many first-time fathers have a hard time accepting that their system is faulty—and that they need to find a better way to schedule the things that really matter.

The List Principle

I BELIEVE IN USING lists to reduce stress. There are dozens of things we could do each day, but we are limited to fitting as much as we can into twenty-four hours. We have to choose the activities that deserve the highest priority. There may not always be time to do everything, but there is always time to do the important things. For me, there is no better way to get things done than by making a list.

Make a list of everything that needs to be done on a daily basis. Include work, housework, your fitness regimen, special projects, and pets that need to be taken care of, among other things. Take a look at your list and determine when you can find time to do these activities. You may not be able to change your work hours, but you can arrange to do the dishes in the morning rather than at night. Instead of cooking meals every evening, you might make them on the weekend, freeze them, and defrost them throughout the week. Be creative. Look at your options and build a schedule that works for both of you.

Daily Activities

_____
_____
_____
_____
_____
_____
_____
_____
_____

Weekly Activities

_____
_____
_____
_____
_____
_____
_____
_____
_____

Monthly Activities

_____

_____

_____

_____

_____

_____

_____

_____

_____

Next, look at each of these sections and rank your activities in their order of importance. Even if you can only complete the "must-do" activities, you will feel more in control.

Sometimes, weekly and monthly activities must be broken down into more manageable chunks. Let's say you have a big project due at work at the beginning of each month. You used to do it the weekend before it was due, but since your baby was born, you can no longer count on this block of time. Instead, you might spend twenty minutes working on it every other night until it's finished.

Using the following worksheets, create a calendar of daily, weekly, and monthly activities for each day of the week.

Monday

Daily Activities

_____
_____
_____
_____
_____
_____
_____

Weekly Activities

_____
_____
_____
_____
_____
_____
_____

Monthly Activities

_____
_____
_____
_____
_____
_____
_____

Tuesday

Daily Activities

_____
_____
_____
_____
_____
_____
_____
_____

Weekly Activities

_____
_____
_____
_____
_____
_____
_____
_____

Monthly Activities

_____
_____
_____
_____
_____
_____
_____
_____

Wednesday

Daily Activities

_____
_____
_____
_____
_____
_____
_____
_____

Weekly Activities

_____
_____
_____
_____
_____
_____
_____
_____

Monthly Activities

_____
_____
_____
_____
_____
_____
_____

Thursday

Daily Activities

_____
_____
_____
_____
_____
_____
_____
_____

Weekly Activities

_____
_____
_____
_____
_____
_____
_____
_____

Monthly Activities

_____
_____
_____
_____
_____
_____
_____
_____

Friday

Daily Activities

_____
_____
_____
_____
_____
_____
_____
_____

Weekly Activities

_____
_____
_____
_____
_____
_____
_____
_____

Monthly Activities

_____
_____
_____
_____
_____
_____
_____

Saturday

Daily Activities

_____
_____
_____
_____
_____
_____
_____
_____

Weekly Activities

_____
_____
_____
_____
_____
_____
_____
_____

Monthly Activities

_____
_____
_____
_____
_____
_____
_____
_____

Sunday

Daily Activities

_____
_____
_____
_____
_____
_____
_____
_____

Weekly Activities

_____
_____
_____
_____
_____
_____
_____
_____

Monthly Activities

_____
_____
_____
_____
_____
_____
_____

Remember, this is only a rough draft. When you use this list for the first time, you'll find things that work and things that don't. Adjust and adapt it until you have created a system that works. If your number one Monday item doesn't get done, move it to number one on Tuesday, and do it before anything else.

A recommendation for fathers who dislike making lists: just try it for a week or two. Who knows? It may work beyond your wildest dreams. Besides, if it drives you crazy, you can always stop using it and come up with a better way that will work for you.

Public Relations

YOU MAY NOT KNOW that, as a parent, you automatically get elected publicity director for your child. This job requires you to protect and enhance your child's image, just as other parents do for their babies. For instance, you will run into people in the supermarket who say that six-month-old Justin is doing long division, or that nine-month-old Amber can recite the Declaration of Independence backwards and forwards.

When this happens, you may look down in your own shopping cart, see little Stevie (who has just mastered drooling), and wonder if you have poor genes or whether you have given birth to Loci, The Goat God. Since neither of these can be true, you may become resourceful when they ask if Stevie sleeps through the night. You know perfectly well that he sleeps two hours at a time, if you're lucky, but there was that one time when he slept almost four hours before waking up—a big improvement, and something that could even happen again. So you nod and say, "Pretty much."

Situations like this always crop up at the most frustrating moments: when your two-year-old is just starting to walk, or when your four-year-old still isn't potty trained. The fact is, everything is relative, and every child develops at his or her own rate.

New Parent Phrases You'll Never Hear

"No she's not walking yet, barely crawling. I think it's a result of poor genes."

"I can't wait for my daughter to grow up and start dating."

"I could listen to the Barney lullaby tape forever. I'm going to get a copy for my car."

"No, we're not taking any pictures of the baby. He's really not much to look at. Do you have any of yours that I could see?"

"No wonder my daughter likes her bottle so much. I tasted her formula the other day, and that stuff is delicious! I bought a couple of bottles for myself to have at lunch."

"We bought a camcorder, but we're waiting until the baby is bigger to see if he does anything interesting. We haven't taken it out of the box yet."

"No, honey, come on. I want to. You got to change her last time."

"I love that 3:00 A.M. feeding. That's when the best shows are on television."

"I wanted to name the baby after my father-in-law, but noooooo, we had to name him after me."

"I like working from home—I can get so much done now."

"My son just loves that bulb syringe. He sees that thing coming and he just laughs and giggles and can't wait for me to stick it up his nose."

Quick Solutions to Little Problems

I have a high-pressure job, and working late makes me feel guilty. But if I take my work home, my wife wants me to take over with the baby for a while.

When you have two kinds of pressure slamming into each other at once, it's time to swap priorities.

When Alex was small, Debbie became stressed out because the housework wasn't done. She can only relax if everything is in order, and she couldn't do the work and take care of the baby, too. At the same time, I was stressed out because a deadline was fast approaching, and I wasn't close to meeting it.

We exchanged priorities. I did everything I could to get the housework done. She made sure I had quiet time to work and that I stayed on top of my deadlines. It worked. By focusing on what the other person was worried about, we took care of both problems.

> *I love my two-month-old baby, but I'm not very involved with him on a personal level. I can't wait for him to grow into a real person. Sometimes I feel like something is wrong with me because my wife and her friends can stare at the baby and talk to him for hours.*

Some people, such as your wife's friends, are baby people, who wouldn't mind if their children stayed babies forever. In fact, some of them go into a baby withdrawal panic as soon as their babies turn two.

Other people, like me, are older-kid people. I enjoyed my sons as babies, but couldn't wait for them to grow up so we could go fishing, play tennis, and knock on doors and run away.

This is very common and nothing to worry about. Simply enjoy the baby stage as much as you can. It doesn't last long.

> *My partner is nursing. I don't feel like I'm playing an active part in the baby's care. I change her, hold her, and that's it.*

Can your partner pump breast milk so that you can feed the baby? Can you supplement the breast milk with formula? Either option would give you more time with the baby and give your partner a break. Also, consider whether you could give the baby a bath or do other activities with him or her during the most active times of the day.

Life in the Blue Banana

NOT SO LONG AGO, Nick learned to recite his full name and other pertinent information.

"What's your name?" we'd ask.

"Nicholas Adam De Morier," he'd state proudly.

"That's right, and what's your address?" And Nick would proudly give his house number and street with a big toothy smile.

Then, we added a new question, "Where do you live?" We thought this was the same question as, "What's your address?" but Nick saw things differently.

"In a blue banana," he'd say. No amount of coaxing or correcting could change this answer.

Life in our blue banana is every bit as strange and unpredictable as you'd expect it to be. We plan about 10 percent of it and wing the rest. The usual rules of logic don't apply here, because we've given birth to a child who doesn't know the rules. How else could you explain why Nick has $10,000 worth of toys, but only wants to play with the turkey baster and drink coasters? By not expecting everything to follow strict rules and procedures, life in our blue banana is more interesting every day.

Crib Notes

Tip #9. Check the diaper bag for diapers.

We tend to think of the diaper bag as more of a survival pack than a place to carry diapers. Ours was filled with cookies, formula, juice, coloring books, a change of clothing, a flare gun, flint and steel, an inflatable raft, and malaria vaccine. Sometimes, the diapers themselves were missing.

Tip #10. Establish a sleep schedule using your internal clock.

If you like to go to bed early and get up early, you take the early morning feeding, and give your wife the ones later at night. If she's breast-feeding and not pumping milk for you to use, she'll need the additional rest. Remember that four to five hours of uninterrupted sleep are better than six or seven fragmented ones.

Tip #11. Do the bills as they come in.

Buy a desk calendar at an office supply store, one where you must turn a page every day, and put it in a safe place on your kitchen counter. As soon as a bill comes in, jot down the due date on the back of the return envelope, postdate a check, put it in the envelope, seal the envelope, and stamp it. Put the envelope on the calendar two or three days before the bill is due. Check the calendar every day for bills that should be put in the mailbox. This will save you time and frustration, and will reduce the chance that you will miss a due date.

Resources

Bliss, Edwin C. *Getting Things Done.* New York: Bantam Books, 1976.

Lamott, Anne. *Operating Instructions: A Journal of My Son's First Year.* New York: Fawcett Books, 1993.

Sears, William. *Keys to Becoming a Father.* Hauppauge, New York: Barrons Educational Series, 1991.

✿ TIPS FROM AUNT IDA ✿

All right, all right. Mickey's a mouse,
Donald's a duck, Pluto's a dog.
What's Goofy?
—Stand by Me

December 29 is a significant date in our family. On that day in history, four-month-old Alex had enough hair on one side of his head to sweep over onto the other side for a true comb-over. Also on that date, Nick made it to the top of the McDonald's Playland Gym and back down again without any assistance from Vestal Emergency Squad 902. (Thanks again, fellas.) And most important of all, December 29 is Aunt Ida's birthday.

Now, Aunt Ida is our family's keeper of all baby knowledge and wisdom. At ninety-five years old, she has acquired several lifetimes of treatments, home remedies, and child psychology. She is half matriarch, half Don Corleone of the family. Her memory is sharp, her voice is loud, and she is quick to share what she knows.

I am forever in my Aunt Ida's debt for my favorite trick, called, "What's that?" When both kids were babies and cried for no reason, I'd ask, "What's that over there?" Even at four months, Nick and Alex would halt their cries long enough to look at the plant, the window, or the calendar on the wall. The change of scenery and change of voice did the job, and they'd forget whatever they had been crying about.

Remember this trick as your kids get older, because it works even better on toddlers. For example, on the days when I wouldn't let Nick have chocolates for breakfast, or when I forced him to wear clothing outside, or imposed some other inhumane atrocity, he'd stomp his feet and cry. I'd say, "Oh, my gosh, what is that?"

"What?" he'd ask, tears running down his cheeks. We'd run into the next room to look out the window. He'd forget to cry as he wondered how Mrs. Parker managed to string Christmas lights on her house without us knowing about it.

I began using this method on Nick when he was six months old, and I will probably still be using it when he is an adult.

"Dad, I can't believe you won't cash in your 401K so I can go with the guys to Vegas!"

"Oh my gosh, Nick, look!"

"What?"

"There's a ferret playing the accordion on top of the garage."

"Where?"

One Year Snapshot

I WANT TO TALK a little about what I like to call non-milestone changes. We tend to look at development as a barometer of our child's intelligence, strength, or character. If little Morgan walks at eleven months, she's gifted, and if she waits until fourteen months, we're concerned that she might end up living with us until she's forty-two.

You'll see developmental charts that show the capabilities children are supposed to have, and the ages at which these developments are supposed to occur. Remember that these numbers are *averages*. Experts add up the ages of millions of children when they first walked, then divide that number by millions of children, and come up with a single age that represents a guess. If you think about it, it's silly to expect that every one of five million babies would all hit a milestone at a certain age. If they did, you'd see this statement in the application requirements for Harvard University: "To be admitted, your child must have crawled at six months, walked at ten months, and talked by sixteen months."

As parents, it's easy to forget this and look at these ages as minimum requirements. Forget the averages, because they aren't important. Only use developmental charts to get an idea of which developments typically happen first.

Here are some non-milestone changes that occur during the first year, and some equipment you may need to prepare for them.

Month One

Changes for Baby	May lift head briefly when on tummy; can focus on a face.
Changes for You	Changes in routine; partner recovering from childbirth; baby needs sponge baths and night feedings.
New Equipment	Crib, bassinet, clothing, changing table, blankets, formula/breast milk, bottles, car seat with carrier that separates from base.

Month Two

Changes for Baby	Umbilical cord falls off; baby eats more and is more alert; first immunizations begin; smiles in response to your smile.
Changes for You	Can give the baby a bath instead of a sponge bath; baby takes more formula/breast milk.
New Equipment	Baby bathtub, easy-enter wind-up swing.

Month Three

Changes for Baby
May start sleeping through the night; doctor may allow the baby to take some cereal; baby may laugh out loud, squeal in delight, and bring hands together; smiles spontaneously.

Changes for You
More sleep; begin spoon-feeding cereal to the baby or giving cereal through a bottle.

New Equipment
Bottles with wider opening for cereal, baby spoon and bowl set, baby seat.

Month Four

Changes for Baby
May be able to eat regular baby food; better head control; may lift head ninety degrees when on stomach.

Changes for You
More time feeding the baby; more interaction.

New Equipment
Bibs, plastic covering for floor while feeding, umbrella stroller.

Month Five

Changes for Baby
Teeth start to come in; baby may have more solid food; may drink juice; may roll over one way; can pay attention to very small objects, reach for an object, and grasp a rattle.

Changes for You
Coping with an irritable baby with sensitive teeth; baby may run low-grade fever while teething.

New Equipment
Training cup, playpen.

Month Six

Changes for Baby	Eats more solid foods; has more regulated sleeping, napping, and eating schedules; might object if you try to take a toy away.
Changes for You	Time for interacting with the baby becomes more predictable.
New Equipment	Walker, high chair.

Month Seven

Changes for Baby	First tooth may come in; baby is more interested in environment; may sit without support.
Changes for You	Interaction with the baby can include reading and singing.
New Equipment	Backpack for carrying the baby, bath seat.

Month Eight

Changes for Baby	Starts to eat finger foods; eats more independently; may become afraid of strangers; may be able to pass an object from one hand to the other and look for dropped objects; can turn in the direction of a voice.
Changes for You	Baby must be introduced slowly to strangers; less time required for feeding, more time required for watching child so he or she doesn't choke on finger foods.
New Equipment	Bigger car seat (when baby is twenty pounds or more).

Month Nine

Changes for Baby	May creep, crawl, or stand; may work to get a toy that's out of reach; may look for dropped objects.
Changes for You	Need to be more alert, as baby is more mobile and curious; install safety locks on doors of cupboards where hazardous materials are stored; put away small or delicate objects.
New Equipment	Outlet covers, locks for cupboard doors, etc.

Month Ten

Changes for Baby	Becomes more interactive; more receptive to conversations, sights, and sounds; may stand while holding onto someone or something, or pull himself or herself up to stand; may say "mama" or "dada" indiscriminately.
Changes for You	Baby's personality develops and attention span grows, so you can read and talk to the child for longer periods of time.
New Equipment	Everything fascinates babies. Pull out your car keys, a pen, a shoe, and watch their eyes pop.

Month Eleven

Changes for Baby	May move away from bottle; becomes more mobile and vocal; begins to associate certain words with objects; understands "no" (but may not obey it); can pick up tiny object with thumb and finger.
Changes for You	Baby spends more time alone studying toys, pots, and pans or watching a special video.
New Equipment	More trainer cups, child-proof dishes.

Month Twelve

Changes for Baby	Baby officially becomes a toddler; is or soon will be walking and talking.
Changes for You	Advance to safety patrol; get in shape by chasing the baby. Can slowly introduce some new foods, including milk and honey.
New Equipment	If baby is walking, parent will need pots of coffee, running shoes, and a catcher's mitt.

Every Baby Is Different

AFTER OBSERVING the difference between my own kids, I can tell you that children's development at various ages is as different as their personalities.

- Alex smiled at two months.
- Nick smiled at two years.

- Nick could fall asleep standing up.
- Alex needed a soundproof room at exactly 68° F.

- Nick's cry most often said, "Get in here, or I'll hurt you when you're old and vulnerable."
- Alex's cry most often said, "I'm really sorry to bother you so late, but when you get a chance . . ."

- Nick screamed.
- Alex sighed.

- Nick slept through the night at ten weeks.
- Alex will sleep through the night before he registers for the draft.

- Alex wants to be the U.S. Ambassador to Thailand.
- Nick wants to be a dump truck.

Child-Proofing Your House

YOU WILL WANT TO child-proof your home to protect your child—and to protect your stuff.

The Basics

- Get plastic covers for electrical outlets that are not in use.
- If the baby is using a walker, make sure stairs are blocked off.
- Use baby-proof cabinet locks for drawers under sinks and for cupboards containing cleaning products.
- Designate one cupboard or drawer for the child's use. Fill it with old pots, pans, plastic bowls, and other child-safe dishes.
- Walk around the house, looking at everything within reach of a baby. Remove anything dangerous or delicate from that level.
- Keep ashtrays out of a toddler's reach. Nicotine from an eaten cigarette butt will make a toddler violently ill.
- Cut drapery or mini-blind cords so they are well out of reach.
- Have the Poison Control phone number posted near the phone.
- Buy syrup of ipecac. The Poison Control Center may direct you to give this medicine to the child to induce vomiting when he or she swallows certain types of poisons.
- Keep houseplants out of reach; some are harmful to small children.
- Put barriers around radiators, heating ducts, or fireplaces.
- If there are tablecloths within a baby's reach, make sure there's nothing on the tables that the child could pull down on top of himself or herself.
- If your child will spend time in other homes, child-proof those, as well.

Never Underestimate the Speed of a Runaway Baby

When Nick was about a year old, he and I were alone in the house one Saturday afternoon. The phone rang, and, as I answered the call, Nick got into my office. He climbed up on my desk chair, got on the desk, and crawled across to the table where my wooden humidor sits. He opened the humidor and discovered the cigars along with a shot glass filled with water (to keep the cigars moist).

The next thing I knew, Nick walked into the living room with the empty shot glass in his hands and said, "All done." My heart leapt to my throat. I knew what nicotine could do to a baby, but I didn't know what stagnant cigar water would do. I got off the phone and called Poison Control, and the nice lady on the other end of the line said, "Well, I've been doing this for seven years, and that's a new one on me."

We were lucky. After twenty-four hours of some interesting intestinal activity, Nick was fine.

When Can Babies Have . . . ?

- **Eggs.** From eight months to a year, depending on the child's allergic reaction to other foods. Most physicians want you to wait until about a year.
- **Milk.** Cow's milk does not have the right mixture of nutrients that an infant needs, and it contains more salt than breast milk or formula. It is not uncommon for infants to have an allergic reaction to cow's milk. Many physicians want you to wait until the first year is over before introducing it into the child's diet.
- **Honey.** As early as eight months. Many doctors recommend that you wait the full year. By then, the child's digestive system is mature enough to handle it.

Babies Should Not Have . . .

- **Smoked or cured meats.**
- **Fish from contaminated waters.**
- **Herb tea.**
- **Coffee, tea, chocolate, soda, or anything with caffeine.**
- **Raw fish, such as sushi.**
- **Vitamin supplements, other than those designed for babies.**
- **Artificial foods (fruit drinks, nondairy creamers, and so forth).**

Home Remedies

AS INTELLIGENT, MODERN individuals, we have a keen grasp of what our children need. We read up on things concerning our children, and if we don't know something, there's always a pharmacist to help us.

Just the same, many of the best treatments for common maladies are of the homemade variety. Simple mixtures from my Aunt Ida's day work at least as well as what is on the market today, often do not contain chemicals or artificial ingredients, and don't have side effects.

For Colic

- **Liquid fennel.** This is probably one of the best natural substances out there for treating colic in babies. It can be purchased in most nutrition stores. Its only side effect: it tends to make the baby sleepy, which, when dealing with an uncomfortable, colicky baby, doesn't seem like a bad side effect at all. You usually place a few drops in the baby's bottle and wait.
- **Rice water.** Although I've never tried this one, I know people who swear by it. Make a pot of rice according to the normal directions, but cook half of the water away. Strain the milky rice water into a bottle and discard the rice. Make sure the rice water is cool before you give it to the baby. Depending on the age of the child, a few ounces can raise any stubborn gas bubble.
- **Rushing water.** Place the baby on a rug on the bathroom floor near the base of the bathtub. Run the bath water. There is something about the sound of the water echoing through the room that often soothes a colicky baby.

For Croup

- **Cold air.** Although everything I've read about croup says to surround the baby with steam, cold air has always worked better for our kids. I often sat on our front porch at 3:00 A.M. with Nick, keeping his body warm and allowing cold air to get in his lungs. Cold air is often better when dealing with a cold or virus as well.

What About . . . ?

- **Crawling.** A baby's knees may become red and sore, especially when his or her legs are exposed. Dress crawling babies in long pants, even in the summer. Also, keep your floors clean. Babies will put large pieces of dirt, pet food, and anything else they find into their mouths.

Watch for the universal sign that something is terribly wrong. When a mobile baby is quiet, you'll inevitably find him or her in the next room, tearing pages from your high school yearbook. As soon as you hear that eerie quiet, grab your emergency gear and find the baby fast.

- **Teething.** Teething babies want to put everything in their mouths, so make sure they only have access to safe items. There are many numbing agents on the market that are designed to take the edge off the pain of teething.
- **Walking.** Babies fall down a lot as they start to walk. You'll want to make sure they aren't practicing near the sharp corners of tables or by the stairs, and that they can't pull anything down onto themselves as they look for ways to pull themselves up.

Development

THE DIAPER CHANGING PROCESS from birth to two years is an excellent example of how quickly babies develop.

- **Changing a child from birth to six months.** Place child on changing table or other flat surface. Unsnap clothes and remove diaper. Wipe area. Dab off umbilical chord. Replace diaper. Replace clothes.
- **Changing a child from six months to a year.** Place child on changing table. Work with rhythm of kicking legs to achieve maximum effect for unsnapping of clothing. Remove clothing. Work with rhythm to replace diaper. Follow this routine while replacing clothing.
- **Changing a child from one to two years.** Stake out area where child may travel regularly; a path to the television or refrigerator is preferred. Remain in stealth position until unsuspecting child comes by. Use military body-tackle to demobilize child. Roll with child and remove shoes and socks. Avoid kicking feet and flailing arms, absorbing any hits in chest and head. Remove child's shirt while holding feet still. Remove old diaper. While child is back on the carpet, use arms and body to hold child's arms and legs still. WARNING—BE PREPARED FOR NAKED ESCAPE. Replace diaper. Replace clothes. Release child back into the wild. Soak your bruises and tend to your wounds.

Crib Notes

Tip #12. *Baby faces.*

Infants as young as two months will react to other babies' faces. There are videos available with soft music and a collection of babies simply cooing and looking into the camera. This will not only soothe and relax the child, but help him or her develop focus and attention.

Tip #13. *Save pop-up books until after the baby is two.*

Although you may think little Bianca would enjoy watching Bambi jump out from the page at her, you can bet that Bambi will be surgically removed from the page in a New York minute, and Bianca will have blood lust for the rest of the forest animals. Put away all of the pop-up books until the child is older and can appreciate them.

Tip #14. *The herb solution.*

How is it that a cold can give a fifteen-pound baby the sniffles and runny eyes, but will knock a hundred-and-fifty-pound adult on his or her back as surely as the Ebola virus? Illnesses from the baby can easily sneak into your adult system, and the next thing you know, pistol-toting bandito germs are riding through the friendly villages of your body, stealing horses and tearing up the saloons.

The best solution to the baby germ war is an herb called echinacea (ek-uh-nay-sha), which can be purchased in any health food store. We start taking it as soon as one of our kids starts to get sick, or whenever we feel like we're coming down with the cold or flu. It doesn't make the cold go away completely, but it does take the edge off it, and gives you a milder, shorter version of the bug. Buy simple echinacea, not echinacea with golden seal or other additives.

Tip #15. *Remember the sunscreen.*

At six months old, babies can and should wear sunscreen. Newborn skin burns easily, especially when exposed to the sun between the hours of 10:00 A.M. and 2:00 P.M. Babies with light hair and eyes are extremely susceptible to sunburn.

Resources

Books

Eisenberg, Arlene, Heidi E. Murkoff, and Sandee E. Hathaway. *What to Expect the First Year.* New York: Workman Publishing, 1996.

Sullivan, S. Adams. *The Father's Almanac.* Garden City, New York: Doubleday, 1992. (This is a great book for games, activities, and toys you can make for your kids out of common household objects.)

Other Publications

MVP Home Entertainment
9030 Eton Avenue
Canoga Park, CA 91304
MVP Home Entertainment is one of the companies that creates videos for babies that include baby faces, dog faces, and cat faces. Both of our kids loved them. Write for a catalog.

Parents Magazine includes monthly tips and stories from other parents, as well as the latest on any manufacturer recalls on baby equipment and other items. To order, call 1-800-727-3682.

HIS THOUGHTS, HER THOUGHTS

A census taker once tried to test me.
I ate his liver with some fava beans and a nice Chianti.
Fuh-fuh-fuh-fuh-fuh.
—Silence of the Lambs

When Debbie and I were dating, we were invited to a nerd party, one of those goofy parties where you and the host are the only ones dressed up, and you spend the rest of the evening wishing that you had left a spare set of clothes in the car. Since embarrassing myself has always been a hobby, I hit a few thrift stores before the party. Six dollars later, I had a pair of plaid pants with an elastic waist, a satin polo shirt with some unidentifiable animal on it, and a great pair of white loafers that looked as if they'd come directly from the collection of Herb Tarleck, the badly-dressed salesman on *WKRP in Cincinnati*. After the party, the nerd clothes were banished to the bottom of a dresser drawer, while I tried to think of a new way to embarrass myself with them.

A few months later, my parents decided to have a lawn sale. They asked if I had anything I wanted to sell, so I brought over the nerd clothes and a few boxes of assorted junk. As my dad went through everything to get it ready for the sale, he found the shoes.

"Hey," he said, excited, checking their size. "These babies are brand new. You can't sell them."

Before I could explain that I'd bought the shoes as a joke, my dad was parading around the living room with his sharp new white loafers, checking himself out in the hall mirror, bending and lifting his heel to test the durability of the sole. His face gleamed, and I caught him cocking his eyebrow and making Clark Gable faces in the mirror. I'm sure he was thinking that it was a good thing he was married, or he could get into some real trouble with those shoes.

Perspective

WHAT WAS GOOFY in my eyes was glamorous in my father's. What I saw as garbage, my Dad saw as a new prize to show off to his pals at the Annex Diner.

Now, this is just a story about the difference in perspective between a father and a son, but we all have stories that show serious differences in perspective between us and our partners. Those differences grow more marked as we graduate to the roles of mother and father.

Fathers and mothers sometimes worry about different things, and they often plan in different ways. This is important to realize, because parenting issues that are crucial to a father may not be at all important to a mother, and vice versa.

For example, my wife moved a great deal when she was a child. Her father's career path called for continual transfers. He would relocate the family every few years or so, and she'd begin life in a new town, a new neighborhood, and a new school. The moves made her uncomfortable. It was difficult to make new friends and adjust. Because of that experience, she insists that our children should have deep roots in one school system.

This reaction is merely Debbie's perspective, a reflection of her own experience. Other individuals with the same background might think that moving frequently was the best experience of their life. They might even want to move their families often, if they believe their experiences taught them to be more outgoing and self-confident.

We all see things a little differently. This is important to know, since we often expect our partners to react to parenting issues the same way we do. Our perceptions have a great deal to do with how we establish our holiday traditions, how we set rules for bedtime, and whether we want the children to call their grandfather Grampy or Pop-Pop. All of these things may be very important to one of us, but mean nothing at all to the other.

Expectations

IF TWO PEOPLE were to experience the exact same thing at the exact same time, they would likely walk away with two completely different reactions. Taking into account individual backgrounds, experiences, fears, lifestyles, goals, drives, and ideas about money, it's easy to understand why your perceptions are so different from your partner's.

Along with all these perceptions come expectations. What do both of you expect the first year of parenthood to be like? How do you see your role? The role of your partner? These are important questions, because, although we rarely discuss our expectations, we feel frustrated when they are not met. If I want to quit my job, open a lemonade stand on the front lawn, and comfortably support our family from the revenue, the flaws in my reasoning will become clear as I discuss these ideas with Debbie.

Your partner may expect that you, the new father, will walk in the door every night at 5:00 P.M., even if you never have done this before. Meanwhile, you might feel compelled to work until at least 7:00 P.M. each night to meet the new financial responsibilities of a baby. In this situation, you and your partner have opposing views of what it means to be a good father.

Here is an opportunity for both of you to articulate what you expect over the next few years. You should each complete the following worksheet separately. When you're finished, compare your answers. Are all of your expectations reasonable? Discuss differences and how to work around them. Then, create a plan that incorporates expectations from both sides.

Activities I expect to do daily:

_____
_____
_____
_____
_____
_____
_____
_____
_____
_____
_____
_____

Activities I expect my partner to do daily:

_____
_____
_____
_____
_____
_____
_____
_____
_____
_____
_____
_____

What I expect my daily routine to be like:

6:00 A.M. _____

7:00 A.M. _____

8:00 A.M. _____

9:00 A.M. _____

10:00 A.M. _____

11:00 A.M. _____

12:00 P.M. _____

1:00 P.M. _____

2:00 P.M. _____

3:00 P.M. _____

4:00 P.M. _____

5:00 P.M. _____

6:00 P.M. _____

7:00 P.M. _____

8:00 P.M. _____

9:00 P.M. _____

10:00 P.M. _____

What I expect to do about night feedings and losing sleep:

_____

_____

_____

_____

_____

_____

_____

_____

_____

_____

Activities I don't mind doing:

_____

_____

_____

_____

_____

_____

_____

_____

_____

_____

_____

_____

Activities I would rather not do:

_____

_____

_____

_____

_____

_____

_____

_____

_____

_____

_____

_____

What I expect to do when I get stressed out or need to relax:

_____

_____

_____

_____

_____

_____

_____

_____

_____

_____

_____

_____

_____

_____

_____

The five most important traditions or beliefs that I would like to pass on to my child are:

1. _____
2. _____
3. _____
4. _____
5. _____

Each of you may see your parental roles differently, but your child will help you sort out who's best at what. At four months, Alex had already picked up on the specific personalities, styles, and mannerisms of his parents. Nick still expects each parent to be in charge of certain activities and procedures. For example, Debbie has to kiss a boo-boo immediately after an accident has occurred. (He will run around with a fork in his knee before he'll let me help.) Once the initial Mommy-kiss has been applied, my kiss can act as a backup, even though Nick knows it contains absolutely no healing power whatsoever.

Mom's Meanings

WE OFTEN EXPECT our partner to understand our meaning rather than our words—and to act accordingly. However, very few people are able to articulate exactly what they mean. Here are common things a new mother may say, and what she really means:

Words	Meaning
How was your day?	Oh god, please talk to me in adult. I'm beginning to think of Barney as a friend.
The baby was a little fussy today.	He took hostages, but I talked him into turning himself in.
I have a job, too, you know!	Remember that scene in *The Untouchables,* with Al Capone and the baseball bat? Huh? Do you?
Will you stay with the baby for a while? I want to run to the store.	Okay, Flight 402 leaves from Gate 4. I catch the connecting flight to Barbados in Chicago.
I never thought it would be like this.	I never thought it would be like this.
Hungry?	The Pizza Hut delivery number is on the fridge.
I can't believe how much money we spend on formula and diapers!	Do they still buy plasma at the blood bank?
I think I'm going to take a bath.	Forget my name. Lose my number. Destroy my file. For the next thirty minutes, I am a ghost. Got it?
I have some pictures of the baby with me, but they're a little old.	This one's from Friday, these are from Thursday, and the ones I took this morning won't be ready until noon.
I'm a little tired today, for some reason.	I'll give you $300 and my wedding ring for another hour of sleep.

Being a Couple While Being a Family

WE NOW HAVE a new person in our lives, our house, our minds, and our ears—something that affects the romantic relationship with our partner. Suddenly, we can't meet after work for a drink anymore, or drop everything and go away for the weekend. We can't even go to the movies or out to dinner without hunting for baby-sitters and packing the diaper bag. Our days of spontaneity seem to be behind us.

In addition, our home may no longer look or smell like the ideal environment for romance. The playpen is now in the living room, the swing is where the stereo used to be, and that charming aroma of Lysol and baby vomit fills the air. Add to this equation sleep deprivation, physical exhaustion, additional work and home pressures, and the fact that a new mother sometimes doesn't feel as attractive or self-confident as she used to, and you have the makings for some interesting relationship changes.

Often, the time we finally can spend with our partner is the off-peak, no-one-else-wants-it, got-a-few-minutes-before-I-pass-out-from-exhaustion time. In our house, that time is after 9:30 P.M. By then, our minds have turned to tater-tots, Debbie can't get the theme song from *The Brave Little Toaster* out of her head, and I'm mentally exhausted from the latest reading marathon of Dr. Seuss' *Green Eggs and Ham*.

This is our convenient couple time, the leftover hour or so when we can possibly have a few minutes of uninterrupted conversation, if we put on a pot of coffee first.

Maintaining a sexual relationship may become an issue as well, because sex with a baby in the house is like living with a time bomb. Tick. Tick. Tick. At any moment, you may hear the detonation, and then, the screaming baby. Of all the romantic, stimulating sounds in the world, a crying baby is just above a garbage disposal, and slightly below any polka. Later, as the baby grows, this explosive becomes a smart bomb, a weapon that is mobile, constantly searching for its target and learning from its mistakes. This bomb could detonate downstairs when little Timmy pulls the toaster on his head, or just outside in the hallway when he's crawled up the stairs and is now trying to open the door, push the dresser back, and get inside the bedroom. So all the rules of spontaneity and crazy whimsical adventure in your sex life must now give way to new strategies and tactics.

- **Create a Sunday afternoon date.** After Nick was born, we began the tradition of taking Nick to his grandmother's for the afternoon. He'd play and take a nap, and we had the entire afternoon to ourselves.

- **Schedule small bits of time for each other during peak times.** Call each other from work just to say hello, send a letter, or e-mail each other. Just a minute or two of time when you're both at your best is equal to a few hours when you'd trade your car for a few extra hours of sleep.

- **Create time for yourselves.** Whether it's going to the movies or sharing a glass of wine in the living room, find time to spend with each other.

- **Begin courting again.** When was the last time you sent your partner a love note? A bunch of flowers or a greeting card mailed to your spouse goes a long way.

- **Budget some of the good time for each other and use the slush time for mundane activities that need to be done.** During peak hours, if you have to choose between mopping the floor, sorting the mail, fixing the toaster, or spending some time with your partner, you know which to do first.

- **Plan your time together.** Do you need time for relaxed conversation? Intimate time? Romantic time? Buddy time? Wind-down time? Decide together and plan accordingly. Fail to plan together, and the first time you have some time away from the baby, you'll come downstairs wearing a Chippendale collar and matching thong while your partner is setting up the Scrabble game and the *Hee-Haw* video.

Be Patient

AS MENTIONED BEFORE, the first year of your child's life will go by fast. The second, third, and fourth years will, too. I remember bringing Nick home from the hospital. I blinked my eyes, and the next thing I knew, Debbie and I were crying because Santa had taken the pacifiers and Nick was now officially a boy instead of a baby. When he goes to kindergarten for the first time, I think we'll need a trauma team standing by.

Be patient, especially during the first few months of the baby's life, when he or she will need all of your attention. Just as you establish a routine that works around the baby's schedule and needs, everything will change again. Eventually, the baby will grow older, times won't be as tough, and you and your partner will have more time together.

Crib Notes

Tip #16. Take videos together.

During the first year of a child's life, there are rarely any videos of the parents without the baby. The baby is the biggest part of your life right now, but you are still a couple. Take a few minutes of couple video to remind you of this.

Tip #17. Develop a stress team.

Talk to your partner about the stress you're going through. Don't worry if it's sounds too technical or too trivial. Sometimes, another person can bring a whole new perspective to the situation.

Tip #18. Have a standing date.

Even if it's only once or twice a month, set aside a time when you can slip out for a cappuccino, go to a movie, or go for a drive. Just an hour or two of together time will make a world of difference.

Tip #19. Give each other a vacation at home.

Take turns taking the baby to visit the family or run errands. This will leave the other parent at home to relax in peace and quiet.

Resources

Coleman, David D., and Diane J. Coleman. *101 Great Dates.* Nashville, Tennessee: Abingdon Press, 1995.

Covey, Stephen R. *The Seven Habits of Highly Effective Families: Building a Beautiful Family Culture in a Turbulent World.* New York: Golden Books, 1997.

Crawford, Debi Dietz. *Advice for a Happy Marriage: From Miss Dietz's Third-Grade Class.* New York: Warner Books, 1997.

DOUBLE INCOME, ONE KID

You know, I started on cleanup, just like you guys.
But now, see, I'm washing lettuce. Soon, I'll be on fries.
Then the grill. A year or two, and I make Assistant Manager.
And that's when the big bucks start rolling in.
—Coming to America

Early on, Debbie and I decided that when we had children, one of us would stay home. I thought it would be me. I had expected to win several Nobel Prizes for Literature by then, and I'd need to stay home to polish them. Then Nick and Alex came along, and I was no closer to winning than making it to the final round of the Publisher's Clearinghouse. Instead, Debbie stays home, and she loves it. A creative, ingenious side of her has come through since she's been a professional mother. Nick and Alex seem quite pleased, as well; they recently gave her a quarterly review, and I've heard they will be picking up her contract for another year.

Staying at home with children today presents a different economic picture than it did in our parents' day. In the early 1960s, for example, the average family income for a young couple with a new baby was around $7,000. Today, it's around $38,000 a year.

Although we may make a great deal more money than our parents did, that money is worth less in real inflation adjusted dollars. In addition, layoffs and downsizing have become more common than in the past, creating new financial concerns for everyone, especially couples with children.

The one-income family is rare today. In 1940, both the husband and wife worked in only 33 percent of all families; in 1994, that figure jumped to 83 percent. In other words, more than three-quarters of all households today have two incomes.

If both parents work, there may be enough money to cover living expenses. But other issues will crop up for working couples with babies.

Quick Solutions to Little Problems

My wife and I both have managerial positions. When the baby is sick and we can't take her to daycare, one of us has to take a sick day and stay home with her. It's always a battle to decide who should stay home.

This is an issue whether both of you are working or not. When my wife is sick, I take a sick day to stay home with the kids. It's just part of the parenting gig.

If both parents work, it's often easiest to take turns staying home with sick children. Consider what's going on at work for both of you. If it's your partner's turn, but she has to make a major presentation in front of three vice presidents and the King of Arabia, it's probably best for you to stay home or find a relative who can help.

When it's your turn to stay home, try to keep the workload from piling up. Make phone calls and try to get some paperwork done. If you have a laptop at home, dial into your work computer and send e-mails.

I work more than forty hours a week. If I don't work late, I have to bring a few hours of work home with me. This means that I never get to see the baby. I feel like a bad father.

This is a time issue, more than anything. To buy yourself an hour or so, try doing your work early in the morning, on the commute to work, at lunch, or after putting the baby down for the night.

If none of these options work for you, it doesn't mean that you're a bad father. Many fathers don't get to spend much time with their children during the week, but they make up for it on the weekend. Those two days belong to their families, and they horde every second of it.

Sure, you'll need to mow the lawn and run errands, but squeeze that in around everything else. Mow the lawn when the baby is napping; take the baby with you when you run errands. Spend your free time with your family. You won't regret it.

We have a colicky baby. We both come home stressed out from work to a baby that cries for hours. I'm afraid one or both of us will have to be committed soon.

There's no definitive answer for this one; not even modern medicine has a precise treatment for colic. The only thing I can say is that it doesn't last.

Take turns with the baby. When it's not your turn, run around the block or get out of the house. Plan meals ahead of time or get takeout so dinner isn't a hassle. Try some of the colic remedies mentioned on page 62.

Stress

HAVE I MENTIONED STRESS yet? How could I be on the seventh chapter of a book about the first year of fatherhood and not have said anything about stress until now? There is no doubt that a baby adds stress to your life. Factor in the stress of your job and other outside irritants, and things really begin to get fun.

Everyone handles stress differently. While some people are able to leave their stress at work, many pack it up and take it home. At home, work stress and home stress are mixed together and lightly simmered.

The way you handle pressure and stress will affect your job, your family, your relationship, and your health. Stress builds up in your body, bubbles in your brain, and slithers into your dreams.

Stress Relievers

There are good methods and bad methods for handling stress. Going to the gym and beating on a heavy bag with your boss's face taped on it would be considered positive. An evening spent guzzling beer until last call at Duke's Bar and Grill may feel great at the time, but the same old issues will be there to greet you the morning after, and you'll wonder where your $300 went (and how to make the room stop spinning).

Physical activity, whether biking up a mountain or cleaning out the garage, is an excellent stress reliever. When we exercise, endorphins are produced in the brain, creating a calming effect. Furthermore, we reduce the physical manifestations of stress, including gastric problems, depression, heart disease, hypertension, and sleep problems.

Having too much to do—and too little time to do it—is a primary cause of stress. Using lists, however, will help you organize your time and prioritize your activities. Write down everything you must accomplish. If you could only finish one thing today, what would it be? Make this your most important goal, focus on it, and finish it. When it's done, cross it off. Then, look at the list again and ask yourself what you'd like to accomplish next. Finish that task while the baby is napping or in the stroller.

Chores

UNLESS YOU HAVE a housekeeper and a live-in cook, there are specific household tasks you'll need to share. If both of you worked before the baby was born, you probably had a somewhat reliable system; if not, you will need to come up with a system now. You've added a new baby to the household, along with about nine thousand new chores.

To create a workable system, write down all the household chores that need to be done. Separate them into daily chores (like cooking, doing the dishes, feeding the baby, and giving the baby a bath), as-needed chores (taking out the garbage and doing baby laundry), and weekly chores (dusting, vacuuming, and cleaning bathrooms).

Next, take turns picking chores that you don't mind doing. When you get down to the last few chores on each list—the worst of the worst—start negotiating. Try your system to see how it feels. You may need to tweak it a little until it works for both of you.

Daily Chores

_____
_____
_____
_____
_____
_____
_____
_____

As-Needed Chores

_____
_____
_____
_____
_____
_____
_____
_____

Weekly Chores

_____
_____
_____
_____
_____
_____
_____
_____

Now, divide up the chores. Take turns choosing from the list above, and write your choices on the worksheets that follow. Make sure all tasks are accounted for.

His Chores

Daily

_____
_____
_____
_____
_____
_____
_____

As-Needed

_____
_____
_____
_____
_____
_____
_____

Weekly

_____
_____
_____
_____
_____
_____
_____

Her Chores

Daily

_____
_____
_____
_____
_____
_____
_____
_____

As-Needed

_____
_____
_____
_____
_____
_____
_____
_____

Weekly

_____
_____
_____
_____
_____
_____
_____
_____

If You Want to Stay Home with Your Baby

IF ONE OF YOU wants to be a stay-at-home caregiver for your baby, either on a part-time or full-time basis, there may be a way. First, think about common reasons for not staying home with the child, then consider your options.

There are generally three reasons why both parents may choose to work full time, instead of having one parent stay home with the baby:

1. Two incomes are required to make ends meet.
2. Two incomes are necessary for the family to maintain its current standard of living.
3. The parents wish to continue building their nest egg.

Let's take a look at each scenario.

Scenario One

We both work because it's a financial necessity.

A household where two people must work in order to meet financial obligations is either a household with too much debt, or a household in which neither wage is sufficient on its own to meet the family's financial needs, even with no debt.

Is your debt too high? Look at your monthly budget. Eliminate the credit card payments, department store payments, car payments, student loan payments, and so on. If you could survive on one income without these payments, you're carrying too much debt.

Reducing debt is a simple and methodical process—we will review the process in greater detail in the next chapter. The basic idea is this: First, prioritize your debts and attack one debt at a time. After you eliminate one debt, roll over the amount you have been paying toward that balance and apply it to your second debt, and so on. The money will snowball as you pick off debts and interest.

If you can't afford to live on a single income, but you would like to find a way for one of you to stay home with the baby, make it your goal to find one job that pays enough to support the family. Setting goals helps you organize your thoughts, create plans, solve problems, overcome obstacles, eliminate worries, and move ahead. People who constantly set and achieve goals make more money, are healthier and more successful, have stronger relationships, experience less stress, enjoy happier marriages, and have nicer teeth. (I have no statistics about the teeth thing—it's just a theory.) There are aisles of books and audio tapes at every bookstore on setting and achieving goals.

Goals will win out over intelligence and talent almost every time. There are three basic types of goals. *Professional goals,* which reflect how we make our living, may involve our present job, the search for a different position, the race to the top, or the building of our own business. *Situation-improvement goals* are objectives we pursue to better the lives of the people in our family. These include establishing a nest egg, taking a dream vacation, or buying a home. *Personal goals* are the things we seek for ourselves: getting in shape, learning a foreign language, taking five points off our golf score, or running with the bulls in Pamplona.

The following is a simple and reliable goal-setting system. One note about goals: you must write them down and continually work at them. A goal that is not on paper is merely a wish.

The Best Goal System Ever

1. State your goal. Write your goal in first person, present tense, and give a specific date for completion. (Example: I will weigh 170 pounds on July 1, 2000.)

_____

_____

_____

_____

2. List twenty benefits you will enjoy if you meet this goal. (Example: If I lose fifty pounds, I'll feel better, have more energy, be more confident, perform better at work, and so on.)

1. _____

2. _____

3. _____

4. _____

5. _____

6. _____
7. _____
8. _____
9. _____
10. _____
11. _____
12. _____
13. _____
14. _____
15. _____
16. _____
17. _____
18. _____
19. _____
20. _____

3. Write down all of the things that could stop you (or already have stopped you) from accomplishing this goal. (Example: I've been stopped because I go out to lunch with the people at work, snack late at night, don't like going to a crowded gym after work, and so on.)

_____
_____
_____
_____
_____
_____
_____
_____
_____
_____
_____
_____
_____
_____

4. Write down ideas for overcoming these obstacles and accomplishing this goal. Then, follow through with your plan. (Example: I'll work out at lunch when the gym is less crowded. That way, I won't be tempted to overeat at noon.)

_____

_____

_____

_____

_____

_____

_____

_____

_____

_____

_____

_____

Scenario Two

> *We could survive with only one of us working, but not at the standard of living we're used to.*

This scenario is better than the first, because if something were to happen to one of your jobs, you could survive on a single income. You have little or no debt, but one income isn't quite enough to take care of the little things that you've come to enjoy.

First, get rid of any remaining debt. Second, analyze your budget. Look for things you can cut back on to make living on one income more comfortable. Focus on what you need, rather than what you want. Finally, consider finding another source of income.

The most obvious way to earn extra income is to build your own home business. It may take a small amount of cash to start, but it will allow one of you to stay home with the baby and still bring in some additional money.

Home-Based Businesses Worth Looking Into

- **A business based on your last position.** Take a set of skills that you've mastered through your previous position and market your services. Become a freelance technical writer, fix computers or VCRs, keep the books for other companies. Use your last position as your qualification for offering the service to others.
- **A business based upon other talents or skills that you have.** Give piano lessons, make homemade baby food, teach a class, make specialized golf clubs—anything where you can translate your talents and experience into part-time income.
- **A business based on a hobby or interest.** If you're going to start your own business, make it fun. Pet sit, write a snowboarding newsletter, create specialized fishing tackle, or restore old books.
- **Other service businesses.** Where you live will determine what types of services are needed, but almost every region has a need for tax preparation, résumé creation, or Internet services.

Home-Based Businesses to Avoid

- **Anything that offers income for manufacturing or assembling products in your home and selling them back to the company.** You will pay a few hundred dollars to buy the materials, and then a few hundred dollars in therapy when you never meet the company standards and are stuck with two hundred jade earrings.
- **Multi-Level Marketing (MLM) opportunities.** Although many of these are legitimate companies that claim to offer a chance to earn a six-figure income, it's best to avoid them. The number of people who actually succeed is small, and the stress of trying to sell, sell, sell to your friends and family is extraordinary. Even if it's the greatest opportunity of the decade, if Jerry from next door keeps his eyes down, runs to his car, and speeds away whenever you're in the vicinity, it's probably not worth it.
- **Any prepackaged business that promises fast, enormous earnings.** If someone is making so much money doing a job like that, why are they telling you about it? Walk away.

Scenario Three

We have very little debt and are building a nice nest egg. If one of us stays home, we'll have to put that on hold. Besides, we will never find jobs as perfect as the ones we have now.

This is probably the best possible financial scenario, and there is only one question you need to ask yourself when deciding whether to continue working or stay home with your child: On a gut level, what feels right? Forget the logical arguments, the advice of your brother-in-law, and the wise words of the guy who fixes the copier at work. Ask yourself, "What feels right?" Your answer will be the right one. Of course, if you don't know what feels right, you need to find out.

Any time that I have ignored my gut feelings, I've regretted it. Whenever I've trusted and acted on them, I've never been disappointed. I've made good decisions by trusting my instincts: I married Debbie; left a job two weeks before I would've been downsized; and returned to the hospital to spend a few more hours with my sister, not realizing she'd die that night.

Don't get instinct confused with psychic ability. Trusting your gut feelings won't help you win the lottery, pick winning race horses, or corner the stock market. It might be difficult to believe instinct even exists if you haven't run the numbers or seen the bottom line. But your own instincts will never steer you wrong, provided you're listening honestly and not trying to steer your feelings toward what you think you should do.

Other Job Options

- **Job sharing.** One full-time position is sometimes split between two part-time workers. A few years ago, this was somewhat rare, and usually limited to the clerical fields. Today, job sharing exists in occupations that range from janitor to senior manager. If you job share with someone, it may be possible to share daycare, as well—a big benefit, since many daycare providers only accept children on a full-time basis.
- **Work at home.** Many companies let employees work at home for a day or two each week. Theoretically, you could make calls

and do paperwork and still throw in a load of laundry between tasks. But don't expect to work eight hours straight when you're taking care of the baby. It is possible to put in eight hours or more of work. However, to do this, you may have to start working several hours before the baby gets up, grab time during the day when the baby is napping, and work a few more hours in the late evening when the baby is sleeping. In spite of the long days, there are advantages. For one thing, you don't have to pay attention to a dress policy. Go ahead and wear the gorilla slippers and old flannel shirt, if you want.

I work best between 5:00 A.M. and 7:30 A.M. I'm a morning person, and this is the time when the house is quiet and my mind is clear. I enjoy working a few hours before Alex starts screaming and Nick walks downstairs with his hair all askew, wanting his juice, his snack box, the *Toy Story* video, and to be left alone. He's a little on edge in the morning.

The last time I tried to do some serious work at home in the middle of the day, it didn't go so well. When Debbie ran to the store, I got involved in a conference call just as Nick decided to see if he could communicate with other planets by screaming. As I was talking to my new boss and a vice president on the cordless phone, holding Nick and listening to him scream, the doorbell rang, and the dog started to bark. At the door, some kid was selling candy bars for his basketball team. It worked out all right for the kid. I tipped him $19.

- **Part-time job.** Take a job part-time, possibly on weekends or a few nights a week. It's a great way to bring in additional income and save on daycare, but you will lose some of alone time with your partner.

The Baby Lobbyists

BE PREPARED to be pressured by other parents about any and all baby issues. There is a political faction of parents who scour the world, recruiting individuals into conversations about such controversial topics as pacifiers, breast-feeding, and whether children belong in daycare. This comes from the black-and-white view that we must make the same decisions for our children that other parents have made for theirs. Otherwise, we might make the wrong decisions. No one wants to be wrong. That's why so many books, magazines, and talk shows present arguments about the "right" way to parent.

Breast-feeding is one of the more controversial issues. To many parents, breast-feeding is great. For one thing, the nutrients and anti-bodies a baby receives through breast-feeding are unique—they aren't duplicated in commercial formula—and they help the baby develop immunities against illnesses. Breast-feeding is cost effective, and it creates a bond between mother and baby. Career women can pump their breast milk and have daycare providers feed it to their babies while they go back to work.

However, as great as breast-feeding is, it is not for everyone. Some mothers can't produce enough milk to satisfy their baby's hunger; they wind up exhausted from feedings that often must take place every hour, on the hour. In this case, it's not worth the mother's sanity to insist that breast-feeding is the only way.

Whether or not to stay home with the baby is another decision that could arouse the hostility of other parents. One of you may find yourself pressured to give up your job, especially if you can survive on one income, but choose not to.

There are benefits to a child staying home with one parent. There are also benefits to putting a child in daycare, where he or she can socialize with other children, or to letting your child spend his or her days with a grandparent or other family member. Do whatever is best for your family. Your decisions may not be right for all families, but they certainly will be right for yours.

Crib Notes

Tip #20. *Talk to each other about your careers.*

Your job, her job, and the parental job are all important, and talking about your jobs will help keep your stress levels down. Besides, your partner may be able to offer insight or a perspective that you haven't thought of yet.

Tip #21. *Save the vacuuming for the weekend.*

On an average weekday, you may have three hours with your child and about the same with your partner. Come home, eat dinner, and make goofy faces at the baby for a few hours. When the baby's in bed, cuddle with or talk to your partner. The dusting and garage cleaning will wait. You won't regret spending those precious hours with the ones you love.

Resources

Goliszek, Andrew. *60 Second Stress Management: The Quickest Way to Relax and Ease Anxiety.* Liberty Corner, New Jersey: New Horizon Press, 1992.

Nelson Bolles, Richard. *The 1998 What Color Is Your Parachute: A Practical Manual for Job-Hunters and Career Changers.* Berkeley, California: Ten Speed Press, 1997.

Peppers, Don. *Enterprise One to One: Tools for Competing in the Interactive Age.* New York: Currency/Doubleday, 1997.

Tracy, Diane. *Take This Job and Love It: A Personal Guide to Career Empowerment.* New York: McGraw Hill, 1995.

CREDIT AND DEBT

Mr. Whicher: *"One outstanding debt to Pacific Bell in the amount of $72.12."*
Mark: *"Oh, but see, that was their fault."*
Mr. Whicher: *"Fifteen bounced checks to this bank."*
Mark: *"Oh, but you see, that shouldn't affect my credit rating because those were just bookkeeping slipups."*
Mr. Whicher: *"What a relief."*
Mark: *"Well, I mean, it's not like I'm poor or something. In all those cases, I had the money, it's not like I couldn't make the payments."*
Mr. Whicher: *"Mr. Watson, I'm going to level with you. This bank is finicky in that when we make a loan, it is important that not only the customer has the money to make the payments, but also, that he or she gives the money to us."*

—Soul Man

For years I said that money was unimportant to me, that the amount of cash I had was not even a minor priority. One day, though, I started wondering why I spent so much money, if it was so unimportant to me. If I didn't need it, why had I gotten myself in such debt? If it wasn't a priority, why was I going through it so quickly? I didn't have much money, so I decided that money had to become important to me. This didn't make me any less honorable or chivalrous or deep. It simply made me more concerned for the freedom, security, and future of my family.

One January, after looking at my income over the past year and realizing how little of it I had enjoyed, I decided that something had to change. Money had to mean something. Once it became important to me, it had value. It became something that shouldn't be squandered, wasted, or misused. It became a tool to help and protect the people I cared about. I wanted my family to be debt free, to save, and to invest in the future. That's what this chapter is all about.

94

Once I became more concerned with money, something strange happened. I spent less time worrying about it. I neither needed nor wasted as much money as before. The more important it became, the less of a burden it was, and the more I enjoyed doing things without it. Up until then, I had made more money than ever before, yet I was up to my neck in debt, with the bulk of my income going out to credit cards, car payments, and other interest-bearing loans. I had little saved and invested, and I was working very hard to make the stockholders of Visa, MasterCard, and Discover quite wealthy.

Credit and debt should be important to every new father for several reasons. How we handle our money today affects the lives of our children, now and in the future. How can we provide for them as babies, toddlers, children, and teenagers to give them the best possible start in life? How can we ensure that we won't be a burden to our children in our golden years? Those tens of thousands of dollars we pay in loan interest every year could become a nest egg for our retirement, our children's education, or funds to start our own business.

When your baby comes, your spending will increase. And as your spending increases, you will want to turn to credit cards. Before you know it, you'll find yourself spiralling into more and more debt.

Credit

IT'S VERY SIMPLE. We establish credit so we can get into debt. But debt is bad, and you can't get more credit if you have too much debt, but you need credit so you can get debt, and credit is good and debt is bad. Got it?

Me neither.

It's not the credit that gets us in trouble, it's the debt. Credit is okay if you use it as a tool, rather than a crutch. Here's an example. Friends of mine charge everything on their credit card throughout the year, because they get frequent-flier mileage and hotel points by using their credit card. They pay the entire balance every month as soon as the bill comes. This method offers big benefits: they never run a balance, they pay no interest, and they get free airline tickets and reduced hotel rates when they fly to New York or Las Vegas for their annual vacation.

Working your credit in this way requires an enormous amount of discipline, but the benefits are worth it. However, some credit card companies are getting wise to this intelligent use of credit, and they will charge a fee if you don't run a certain balance throughout the year. Stay away from these, if you can.

Three Uses for Credit

- **To charge perishables.** This is the worst use of credit. It makes no sense to charge meals that you'll eat in an hour. If you pay the minimum every month, it may take months or years to pay off food that you enjoyed for just a few minutes.
- **To charge depreciables.** This is a little better, but not much. Depreciables include furniture, clothes, and other things that will last a little longer than food. The interest on depreciables is a huge drain on your finances. If you pay the minimum amount each month, you'll end up paying two to three times the value of the item by the time it's paid off.
- **To purchase appreciables.** This is the best use of credit. Appreciables are your home, real estate, and other assets. With a mortgage, for instance, you will still pay interest rates, but the item will increase in value over time.

Credit tips

- **Use store layaway plans instead of credit cards.** You'll pay a little at a time and have your merchandise in a few weeks. Try to find a store that has no layaway fee; that way, you pay only the ticket price for the item.
- **Avoid thinking of purchases in terms of monthly payments.** That $17 minimum payment will drag on forever, and the total will add up fast when $15.75 of it is interest. The way to get around this is to multiply the payments by the length of time you'll be paying them. Then ask yourself if what you're buying is really worth what you're actually going to be paying for it.
- **Use your credit card wisely.**

The Best Ways to Use a Credit Card

1. As month-long, interest-free loans. Charge if you must, but pay the entire balance when the statement comes.
2. To collect frequent-flier miles, car points, and other discounts while not running a balance.
3. For emergencies. Again, if you charge anything, pay off the entire balance at the end of the month.

The Worst Ways to Use a Credit Card

1. To buy the things you want, but can't afford.
2. To get cash advances whenever you feel like it.
3. To charge meals and other perishables. These will be a distant memory long before you pay off the charge.

Establishing Credit

ESTABLISHING CREDIT IS really quite simple, because credit institutions are more than happy to give it to you. These companies grant credit to individuals based on past credit history, employment, income, and outstanding debt.

If you have no credit history, you can develop one fairly quickly. If you've been in a mall in the last twenty years, you can barely take a step without someone offering you 10 percent off your purchase if you apply for the store's charge card. The next time this happens, take them up on it. Charge something small, and pay it off as soon as the bill comes. Now you have a perfect credit history.

If you're after a larger loan, such as a mortgage, you'll have to develop more of a credit history. Paying off the Sears charge that you just opened last month might not be enough to impress the mortgage company, but it should be enough to impress the folks at Visa, MasterCard, and Discover. With a few of these under your belt, you'll be on your way.

What People Look for When Deciding to Grant You Credit
(in order of importance)

1. A home with a mortgage.
2. An American Express card or Diners Club card.
3. A job you've had for a year or more.
4. A bank loan that's been paid off or is up to date.
5. A Visa or MasterCard.
6. A department store card that is paid off or in good standing.
7. A telephone in your name.

Repairing Credit

A POOR CREDIT RATING is often not very difficult to repair, and it should be fixed, even if you don't need the credit. Many prospective employers check credit reports to see how responsible a candidate is. Even if you are resolved never to charge anything again for the rest of your life, so help you God, you still need to repair that credit rating.

First, get a copy of your credit report. The credit reporting industry is dominated by three main corporations: Experian (formerly CCN Group and TRW Information Systems & Services), Trans Union, and Equifax. Experian offers one free credit report a year, but it covers only a portion of your credit history. When applying for a mortgage or other large loan, the lending agency will request a full factual file, which is a report from all three companies. Your full factual file will list all current and past debt and your payment history. In order to see your complete credit history, you'll need to contact Equifax and Trans Union and request an application from them, as well.

Once you receive your credit reports, check them for errors. These companies issue more than one million credit reports every day, and are not always timely about correcting errors and updating information. In fact, a study done in 1979 by The Givens Group showed that twenty-four out of twenty-five credit reports had incomplete or inaccurate data. If your credit reports are wrong, follow the instructions for making corrections.

When you're satisfied that your credit history is accurate, turn to your outstanding debt. If you have overdue debt, take care of that first. Contact the holder of the loan and arrange a payment schedule or see if they will settle for half or even a third of what you owe. Lenders of guaranteed loans for students will not settle for anything less than the full amount owed, but many banks and credit card companies have been known to negotiate.

When negotiating to pay off an old debt, try to get the institution to refer to the debt as a *non-rated loan* on your credit report. A non-rated classification will take away the overdue status of the debt. Your report will show that no money is due, so it will be in neither good nor bad standing. If you do have any bad ratings, it will take three years for them to be removed from your credit report.

Debt

ON AVERAGE, A THIRD of each paycheck goes to taxes, and another third to interest and debt. This means that most people use only one-third of their income to buy food and clothing, to invest, to spend on vacations, to raise their family, and to retire on.

Imagine for a moment that you are completely out of debt and own your home outright. One-third of your income would go toward taxes, and one-third would go toward food, clothing, gasoline, utilities, and so forth. This frees up one-third of your income to put toward investments.

Take this example one step further. If you need $1,000 a month to cover your expenses, and your investments produce $1,000 in interest every month, what could you do? Anything you wanted to.

Impossible, you say, to have a large enough investment portfolio to produce $1,000 a month in interest? Did you know that a portfolio of $125,000 would accomplish this feat? Now, $125,000 may seem like an enormous amount of money that would take a lifetime to acquire. Consider this: if a couple making $35,000 a year is debt free, and if they invest $800 a month at a return rate of about 12 percent a year, the couple would have $125,000 in less than eight years.

Here are the basics of turning your money situation around: 1) get out of debt, 2) invest the money with which you would normally pay off your debts every month, and 3) use cash to buy what you need or want (you can use a credit card, but be sure to pay off your monthly balance). At this point, it may seem impossible to squeeze an extra dime out of your check to pay off anything, but I can almost guarantee there's a way. To do it, you must either devise new ways to save money, or find money somewhere in your budget.

Saving Money

Regardless of whether or not you're carrying debt, there are ways to save money in the first year of parenthood.

- **Join a warehouse club.** Stores such as Sam's Club and Cosco are great places to stock up on items like bulk diapers and baby wipes, and at a lower cost than you'd find in traditional stores.
- **Don't buy diapers in grocery stores.** On the whole, grocery stores charge $.20 to $.25 more per diaper than department stores or pharmacies.
- **Make your own baby food.** This may sound difficult, but it's incredibly easy. Cook peaches, carrots, squash, a banana, or other food and mash them up in a food processor. Scoop the mashed fruits and vegetables into ice cube trays, freeze, pop the little cubes into freezer bags, and you're all done. When it's time to eat, just put them in the microwave and heat them. It usually takes about thirty minutes to make a month's worth of food, and it costs just pennies.
- **Shop for baby furniture at a department store or furniture store rather than a baby store.** If you need a dresser or a night stand, you can find one in a furniture store for as little as $80. The same quality dresser in a baby store might cost $150.
- **Check out garage and yard sales.** These are often loaded with baby bargains, from furniture to clothes.
- **Buy refillable packages.** A refill of diaper wipes, for example, costs 25 percent less than a new box. Simply pop the refill wipes into the old box.
- **Get a free car seat.** Last time I checked, Midas Muffler and Brakes offered a car seat at the wholesale cost of $42. When the baby outgrows the seat, you take it back and get a $42 gift certificate for auto repairs.
- **Buy generic brands.** In most cases, diaper creams, lotions, and baby shampoos are exactly the same as name brands, but they cost a third less.

- **Buy day diapers and night diapers.** Buy premium-brand diapers for the nighttime, when the baby will be in the diaper longer, and buy middle-of-the-road brands for the daytime, when the baby is in the diaper for just a few hours at a time. WARNING: Avoid the ultra-cheap diapers. Some of these are so thin that you'll be changing the baby three times as often, and will actually end up spending more.
- **Cut coupons.** You can save up to 30 percent by using manufacturer and store coupons. With just fifteen minutes of effort, you could save as much as $25 a month. Multiply this by four, and that's $100 an hour for your trouble. Some manufacturers will give you coupons if you request them.
- **Stockpile.** Whenever there's a sale on diaper wipes, buy six boxes. You can use these until they go on sale again.
- **Use rebates.** Many people get sucked into buying a product by the rebate price, but never get around to sending in the rebate, so they end up giving that money to the manufacturer. As with coupons, just a few minutes of effort can pay off.
- **Save manufacturer coupons until you see the item on sale.**
- **Buy in bulk.** You can often save up to 30 percent by buying larger boxes or bottles, but not always. Check out the price per serving of the smaller item, do the same for the larger item, and compare the two prices.
- **Plan meals ahead of time.** You're more likely to stick to a plan, and you won't waste as much of the vegetables and fresh produce you buy.
- **Make large meals and take leftovers for lunch.** A cold sandwich doesn't always hit the spot, especially on a cold, snowy, dreary day at the office, but heating up a casserole is a different story.
- **Avoid baby life insurance.** Unless your baby is the next Pampers model and will be supporting the whole family, baby life insurance is a waste. Disability insurance for the primary wage earner is a smarter buy.

Finding Money in Your Budget

List everything you buy over a week's time. Don't punish yourself, just list every lunch, cup of coffee, newspaper, take-out, and so on. At the end of an average week, list all the common denominators. If you buy a cup of coffee, a bagel, and a newspaper on the way to work every day, it can easily rack up to $60 a month. Some of this money can be put toward your debt. Now don't go giving up all the little things you enjoy, just because they're not absolutely necessary in your life. First of all, there's no need, and second, it rarely works. Some of us would rebel if we couldn't have our cherished newspaper or bagel every day. But if you think you can go without buying your morning cup of coffee, that money is now available for debt reduction.

Getting Out of Debt

THERE ARE TWO basic methods of reducing debt, and both require the same first step: List all the debts you are carrying, the time left on each loan (or, in the case of credit cards, the time left if you make minimum payments), and the interest you are being charged for each.

Example

Car

Amount	$15,000
Interest Rate	7.9%
Years Remaining	4 years
Monthly Payment	$365.49
Total Interest	$2,543.53

Furniture

Amount	$2000
Interest Rate	21%
Years Remaining	5 years
Monthly Payment	$54.11
Total Interest	$1,246.30

Credit Card

Amount	$5,000
Interest Rate	15%
Years Remaining	8 years*
Monthly Payment	$90.00*
Total Interest	$3,589.36*
Total Interest	$7,379.19

*Assuming that minimum payments are made.

Method One

Let's say that by using cost-cutting strategies and eliminating unnecessary expenses, you are able to set aside $50 a month. You could put this money toward your debt reduction plan. Here's how.

After listing your debts (using the example above), target the debt with the shortest remaining loan life. Send your extra $50 a month to that debtor until the debt is paid off. Using the previous example, you would start first with the car loan, making a monthly payment of $415.49 (the minimum monthly car payment of $365.49, plus the $50). By making a higher monthly payment, your total interest paid would equal $2,183.89 (a savings of $359.64), and you would pay off the loan six months early.

When the car loan is paid off, take the money you used for your monthly car payments and add it to your monthly furniture payments. Your furniture payments become $469.60 a month ($415.49 from the car, plus $54.11 for the furniture). You would make your last payment sixteen months early, and you would pay $1,122.80 total in interest (a savings of $123.50).

Finally, apply the $469.60, which you had been paying for furniture, to the remaining balance on your credit card. With monthly payments of $559.60 ($469.60 from the furniture, plus $90 for the credit card), you would pay off your final loan forty-four months early, and the interest would total $2,516.02 (a savings of $1073.34).

By using this method, you would be out of debt almost four years early and save $1,556.48 in interest.

Method Two

Rank your debts by rate of interest and apply the extra $50 to the debt with the highest interest rate. In this case, you would focus on the furniture first, making monthly payments of $104.11 ($54.11 plus the $50). You would make your last payment thirty-six months early, and the interest would total $459.15 (a savings of $787.15).

The credit card comes next. Add the money previously used to pay off your furniture loan ($104.11) to the remaining balance on the credit card ($90), making your monthly payments $194.11. Your last payment would come forty-five months early, and your interest paid would total $2,137.33 (a savings of $1,452.03). By now, the car would have been paid off two months ago. You would be out of debt almost four years early, saving $2,239.18 in interest payments.

Comparing these two methods of debt reduction, you would save $682.80 more in interest by using the second method. This is almost always the case when your debts have varying interest rates. If the interest rates are closer together, the advantages of the second method will not be as dramatic.

In many cases, however, there is a psychological advantage to using the first method over the second. If you can pay off three or four small debts by using the first method, that sense of accomplishment may give you the momentum you need to continue reducing your debt.

The Real Savings

If you take this exercise one step further, you will see an even greater advantage to getting out of debt fast. If you are out of debt four years ahead of time, you'll be able to save an extra $559.60 a month— money to be put toward your investment portfolio. At the end of four years, you will have set aside $26,860.80. Add in the interest you've saved by paying your debts early, and you've pocketed nearly $30,000—and that doesn't include the return on your $559.60 a month investment.

Now it's your turn. Fill in the following two worksheets with your debt information. In the first, rank your debts by the remaining life of the loan (shortest to longest). In the second, rank your debts by interest rate (highest to lowest).

To plan your debt reduction, look at the worksheet for method two. If your interest rates vary widely, use method two to reduce your debt. If the interest rates are about the same, use whichever method you prefer.

Method One Worksheet

Debtor	Total Debt	Amount Paid Each Month	Months Remaining	Ranking

Method Two Worksheet

Debtor	Total Debt	Amount Paid Each Month	Interest Rate	Ranking

There is an exception to the get-out-of-debt-fast rule. If the interest rate you are being charged on a debt is lower than the rate you can yield on an investment, put the money into the investment. In other words, if you have to choose between investing money into a savings account at 5 percent interest, or paying off your student loan at 3 percent interest, you're probably better off leaving the student loan unpaid.

Crib Notes

Tip #22. Ride the full month on your credit cards.

If you're going to use a credit card, get the maximum use before the interest begins to accrue. Find out when your billing date is, and charge just after that date. If your billing date falls ten days into the month, and you charge on the 1st, you only have two weeks before that charge is billed. But if the billing date falls the 10th, and you charge on the 12th, you will use their money for a longer period of time before accruing interest. (This does not apply to cash advances, which start accruing interest the day you use them.) Make sure you have a card with a grace period and no annual fee.

Tip #23. Get an American Express Card.

If you're going to use credit cards, get an American Express Card (or a card that makes you pay off the balance every month). The $55 you pay in maintenance fees will be a lot less than the interest payments you would make on another credit card.

Better yet, use a debit card. A debit card looks like a credit card, but actually draws money directly from your checking or savings account. Be sure to get a debit card without a cash reserve, so you can't spend more than you have in your account.

Tip #24. Deduct the charge in your check register.

Every time you charge something, think of that money as already gone. Write a check to pay it off as soon as you get home.

Resources

Books

Fields, Denise, and Alan Fields. *Baby Bargains: Secrets to Saving 20% to 50% on Baby Furniture, Equipment, Clothes, Toys, Maternity Wear and Much, Much More!* Boulder, Colorado: Windsor Peak Press, 1997.

Hammond, Bob. *Life Without Debt: Free Yourself from the Burden of Money Worries Once and for All.* Franklin Lakes, New Jersey: The Career Press, 1995.

Credit Report Information

To request your free credit report from Experian, call 1-800-392-1122.

To request a credit report application from Equifax, call 1-800-685-1111. The cost is $8, and processing usually takes about three weeks.

Trans Union provides free credit reports to consumers who have been denied credit, insurance, or employment because of information on their credit report (or for other legal reasons). There is a nominal fee for other requests.

To request a credit report application from Trans Union, write down your first, middle, and last name (including Jr., Sr., and III); current address; previous addresses in the past two years, if any; social security number; date of birth; current employer; phone number; and signature. Send these to:

Trans Union Corporation
Consumer Disclosure Center
P.O. Box 390
Springfield, PA 19064-0390

Money Savers

Your Daily Freebies offers links to all the best free stuff on the web. Go to: (http://members.tripod.com/~SJEWELRYS/shopper3.html). Updated daily!

Companies with New Parent Programs (free merchandise and coupons):

Baby Magic	1-800-228-7408
Beechnut	1-800-523-6633
Johnson	1-800-BABY-123
Evenflo	1-800-233-BABY
Fisher Price	1-800-432-KIDS
Gerber	1-800-443-7237
Growing Healthy Brand Baby Foods	1-800-755-4999
J & J	1-800-526-3967
K-Mart (Baby of Mine Club)	1-800-533-0143
Lactaid	1-800-HELP-KIT
OshKosh B'Gosh	1-800-282-4674
Similac/Ross Laboratories	1-800-BABYLINE
Zilactin Extra Strength (teething gel)	1-800-746-8888

♺ BUDGETS ♺

C'mon, do I look like the mother of the future? I mean, am I tough?
Organized? I can't even balance my checkbook.
—The Terminator

In commercials, television shows, and casual conversation, every-one seems to talk about "sticking to their budget." In most cases, they're simply talking about what they can afford. Few people have an actual working budget—it seems too complicated.

In reality, a budget is nothing more than a summary of how much cash is coming in and how much is going out. Your household may seem far away from the cold world of business, but both entities buy materials, borrow money, pay utilities, and cover maintenance costs. They both try to show a profit every year, and, if they don't, costs must be cut or productivity increased.

You might be a financial genius making millions of dollars a year, but if you don't use a budget, you are not in control of your personal finances. A budget is the best way to track income, investments, and financial obligations. It represents your business, with your household as the corporate headquarters. Where does the bulk of your income originate? How effectively is it utilized? Where can costs be reduced? What methods are in place to increase profits and keep costs down?

Budgeting for the First Time

CREATING A BUDGET means comparing a list of your annual expenses to your annual income. An accurate budget will include all expenses, even those that are months away from being due.

Expenses

To keep track of expenses, it is often helpful to separate them into categories. There are three categories of expenses.

- **Fixed expenses** are the same each month. These include rent, mortgage, and car payments.
- **Variable expenses,** such as groceries, gasoline, and entertainment, fluctuate from month to month.
- **Periodic expenses** occur annually, semi-annually, quarterly, or at other predictable times, and include insurance premiums and property taxes.

1. **To determine your annual expenses, first list all of your fixed household expenses for one month.**

Monthly Fixed Expenses

Expense _____ $ _____

Expense _____ $ _____

Expense _____ $ _____

Expense _____ $ _____

Expense _____ $ _____

Expense _____ $ _____

Expense _____ $ _____

Expense _____ $ _____

Expense _____ $ _____

Total $ _____

2. Next, list your variable expenses. If you don't have a regular bill for groceries, gasoline, or other variables, choose an amount that seems reasonable. Adjust it over time to make it one you can live with.

Monthly Variable Expenses

Expense _____ $ _____
Expense _____ $ _____
Expense _____ $ _____
Expense _____ $ _____
Expense _____ $ _____
Expense _____ $ _____
Expense _____ $ _____
Expense _____ $ _____
Expense _____ $ _____

Total $ _____

3. List periodic expenses that come up throughout the year. Be sure to include birthdays, holidays, vacations, and other expenses.

Periodic Expenses

Expense _____ $ _____
Expense _____ $ _____
Expense _____ $ _____
Expense _____ $ _____
Expense _____ $ _____
Expense _____ $ _____
Expense _____ $ _____
Expense _____ $ _____
Expense _____ $ _____

Total $ _____

4. Multiply your total fixed and variable expenses by twelve, then add these numbers together, along with your periodic expenses. The grand total represents your annual expenses.

$$\text{Fixed expenses (x 12): } \$ \underline{\hspace{2cm}}$$
$$\text{Variable expenses (x 12): } \$ \underline{\hspace{2cm}}$$
$$\text{Periodic expenses: } \$ \underline{\hspace{2cm}}$$

$$\text{Grand total: } \$ \underline{\hspace{2cm}}$$

5. Finally, divide the grand total by the number of times that you are paid in a year. If you're paid once a week, divide by fifty-two; if every other week, by twenty-six, and so on. In order to meet your expenses, you will need to set this much aside from every paycheck.

$$\text{Grand total} \div \text{(paychecks per year)} = \$ \underline{\hspace{2cm}}$$

6. This is the amount you must reserve from every paycheck in order to pay your expenses. If your expenses exceed your income, you must either find an additional source of income, or adjust your standard of living.

Making Changes to an Existing Budget

IF YOU HAD a working budget before the baby was born, you'll need to add in new expenses to cover the cost of a child. List the amounts needed to pay for diapers, formula, baby food, and other items. You may need to tailor your budget toward one of the following models.

- **Debt Reduction Budget.** As explained in the last chapter, you can rank your debts according to either their interest rates or the time remaining on each loan. In a debt reduction budget, you'll focus on one debt until it is paid off, then you will attack the next debt, and so on, until all your bills are paid off.
- **Savings and Investment Budget.** Use this budget when you are out of debt and ready to put money into either an investment portfolio or a large cash purchase (to pay for a car with cash, for example). The key to a savings and investment budget is to treat

the money going into your portfolio as a bill. This is money owed to your family, and it must be paid every month.

- **The "One of Us Should Be Able to Stay Home" Budget.** This budget, too, should be used only after reducing or eliminating your debt. If there is not enough income for one of you to stay home with the baby, you'll need to either create a second source of income through your investment package, or set aside a stockpile of cash for expenses. See pages 85 through 91 for ideas on how to do this.

Adjusting

Your budget will probably take a month or two of field-testing before it goes smoothly. There will probably be things you left out, underestimated, or misjudged. Once you see what works and what doesn't, you'll be able to adjust your budget to fit your needs. When you finally get your budget just right, it'll be time to change it again. Formula gives way to baby food, and baby food to school lunches, and suddenly you've promised little Jake that you'll take him to SmartPlay every Sunday afternoon, or have a movie night with pizza and popcorn on Fridays. As your child grows and your family grows, your budget will need to change.

Quick Solutions to Little Problems

What if we finish our budget and have a large amount of money left over?

This is a nice problem to have—if it's for real. Finances generally look better on paper than they do in practice. We often forget the smaller expenses, such as coffee, newspapers, and bagels on the way to work. We might even forget to account for a large debt or periodic expenses that are coming up later in the year.

Take a closer look at your budget and see if anything has been missed. If everything looks all right, try the budget for a few months. See if you really have $300 left over at the end. If not, find out where that money is going.

What if, according to our budget, we need more money than we have coming in?

If your expenses are greater than your income, you are living beyond your means. Take a step back and re-evaluate your priorities. You can only live beyond your income for so long before you'll have an enormous pile of debts with no way to pay them off.

Electronic Budgeting

IF YOU DON'T TRUST your math skills, there's plenty of budgeting software on the market today. Quicken dominates the home-budgeting software world, with Microsoft Money running a close second. Quicken sells for between $19.95 and $100 ($39 is the average) and is available for both Macintosh and PC. It does everything from balancing your checkbook to monitoring your savings and investments. With Quicken 6.0, you have the option of paying your bills and doing your banking online. Even someone with absolutely no understanding of accounting can use it effectively.

Microsoft Money does everything Quicken does, but has some advantages overall. Switching to different screens is easier, and the financial calculators are more advanced. Using these calculators, you can experiment by adding various amounts to monthly loan payments to see how much interest you can save. You can also set a savings goal and see how long it will take to reach it, taking into account varying interest rates and monthly contributions. Finally, you can amortize mortgage and other debt payments for faster payoffs. Microsoft Money runs around $30 or less.

Cash Graph, Inc. has come up with a unique approach to budgeting software. Rather than offer customers useless or frivolous extras, Cash Graph sells three separate software packages, each of which focuses on a specific aspect of home budgeting. There is Cash Graph Checking for basic budgeting and bills; Cash Graph Personal Inventory for investments, savings, and other financial goals; and Cash Graph Appointment for time management. Each package runs around $10.

Budgeting electronically promises greater accuracy, as well as the convenience of having all your financial information and history at your fingertips. This feature is worth its weight in gold at tax time each year. Quicken, like other accounting packages, keeps track of tax-related accounts and can generate reports that tell you which totals go where and on what form. And if you update your version every year, which is usually less expensive than buying a new package, you can do your own taxes. Quicken even prints out the forms. All you have to do is enter your account and checkbook information, and the program does the rest. Of course, using accounting software does require some maintenance time to keep your financial records entered and up-to-date in the computer, but the time you'll save at the end of the year is well worth it.

Crib Notes

Tip #25. *Give yourself an allowance.*

When Debbie and I first got married, things were a little tight. Once we paid our bills, I had $7 a week for myself, which lasted about seven seconds.

After we paid off a few loans, my spending money went up to $12 a week, then $20, then $40, but no matter how much I had, it only lasted about seven seconds. Usually, I spent it all without thinking on car washes, lunches, newspapers, and other things that came up throughout the week.

Try to budget for minor expenses that might arise on a regular basis, and be sure to allow yourself a specified amount of money that you can spend any way you want to.

Resources

Dominguez, Joe, and Vicki Robin. *Your Money or Your Life: Transforming Your Relationship With Money and Achieving Financial Independence.* New York: Penguin, 1993.

Loungo, Tracy. *10 Minute Guide to Household Budgeting.* New York: Macmillan General Reference, 1997.

Peetz, Tuttie. *Basic Budgeting and Money Management: A Guide for Taking Control of Your Spending.* Carlsborg, Washington: Systems Co., 1996.

🍂 SAVING AND INVESTING 🍂

Josh: *"Turns out Dad is a financial genius."*
Dad: *"Oh, all I did was take the money you sent home and embark on a periodic investment in a no-load mutual fund."*
—The Jerk

It would take several books to present all the information you would need to create a solid savings and investment plan. At the same time, no book on becoming a new father would be complete without a discussion of this topic, since it forms the basis of how the present and future needs of your family will be met. Your careers, of course, should offer a steady increase in income over time, but with a new baby in the family, you and your partner must come up with a strategy to maximize the money you have. The decisions you make could determine the kind of education your children receive and what their earning potential will be.

The information in this chapter is intended to help you start thinking about saving and investing. The main idea is to develop a plan, either on your own or with the help of a professional financial planner. As a couple, you may have gone without such a plan, but as parents, you must live up to the responsibility of ensuring your children's future.

And make no mistake, that future is going to cost money. The Family and Economics Research Group estimates that it takes $334,000 to raise a child from birth to age seventeen—and that doesn't include college or a car. That's almost $20,000 a year until the child goes to college—and then the *real* expenses begin. Statistics also show that 24 percent of all grown children come home to live with their parents at least once in their lifetime, often bringing their own children with them.

You can see why you'll need a plan. Unless you expect to quadruple your income soon or become fabulously wealthy by noon tomorrow, you'll need to look at your present income, expenses, investments, and savings to figure out how you'll fund these expenses. You'll need to cover tuition costs, as well as those $1,200 sneakers your kids will absolutely need. And maybe, just maybe, you'll even figure out a way to do all this and still retire before you're ninety years old.

An Income Plan

YOU CAN MAKE ALL the grandiose plans in the world, have zero debt, and research all the latest techniques for investing and saving, but unless you have a strong and steady flow of income (or win the lottery), none of it will matter. Solid career goals, including income estimates for the next five, ten, and fifteen years, are critical. If you allow luck to decide your career path, luck will also determine your financial path.

Income from you and your partner over the next twenty or thirty years will form the foundation of your financial plan. You may expect to stay with your company until they drag you out of your office, kicking and screaming. But remember, we live in a volatile age. Downsizing, layoffs, mergers, and acquisitions are common. You'll not only need a plan for the future, but you'll want to have a backup plan as well, in case the fates deliver a body tackle along the way.

The following questions will help you think about your career and the direction you want it to go in the future. It will also help identify some of the expenses you will need to include in your expense plan. Both you and your partner should think about and answer these questions.

1. Realistically, how much money do you expect to make in five, ten, and fifteen years?

	You	Partner
Five years	_____	_____
Ten years	_____	_____
Fifteen years	_____	_____

You may want to contact the personnel department at your work to find out the range of annual pay increases for your job classification. Be sure to take into account any promotions you anticipate. Your local career center, too, may be able to help you estimate pay rates if you are thinking of changing careers.

2. Do you expect to be working for the same employer in ten years?

	You	Partner
Yes	_____	_____
No	_____	_____

3. If so, do you plan to move up the career ladder there?

	You	Partner
Yes	_____	_____
No	_____	_____

4. Would you like to be working in a different field in ten years?

YOU

Yes _____ No _____ If so, which one?

What education or training will you need?

How long will it take to complete the education/training?

How much will it cost?

PARTNER

Yes _____ No _____ If so, which one?

What education or training will you need?

How long will it take to complete the education/training?

How much will it cost?

5. **Will you be self-employed in ten years?**

YOU

Yes _____ No _____ If so, in what business?

Will you start working part-time, then move to full-time as the business grows?   Yes _____ No _____

What education or training will you need?

How long will it take to complete the education/training?

How much will it cost?

PARTNER

Yes _____ No _____ If so, in what business?

Will you start working part-time, then move to full-time as the business grows?   Yes _____ No _____

What education or training will you need?

How long will it take to complete the education/training?

How much will it cost?

6. Will your career or goal require further education?

Yes _____ No _____

When will you go back to school?

What education or training will you need?

How long will it take to complete the education/training?

How much will it cost?

Does your employer offer tuition reimbursement?

Yes _____ No _____

Yes _____ No _____

When will you go back to school?

What education or training will you need?

How long will it take to complete the education/training?

How much will it cost?

Does your employer offer tuition reimbursement?

Yes _____ No _____

If your employer offers a tuition reimbursement plan, remember that most of these programs require you to pay your own tuition up front and receive a passing grade in the class before you are reimbursed.

7. Will you move to another geographical area in the next five, ten, or fifteen years? (To be completed as a couple.)

Yes _____ No _____

If so, how long will it be before you move?
Five years _____ Ten years _____ Fifteen years _____

How much will it cost you to move?

How much do rent/mortgage, heat, electricity, and other utilities cost in your current home?

How much will rent/mortgage, heat, electricity, and other utilities cost in your new home?

Expenses

THE LAST CHAPTER discussed budgets, expenses, and strategies for saving. Now we'll take it to the next level. Just as your income will change over the next five, ten, and fifteen years, so will your expenses. The following questionnaire will identify areas where some of these changes might occur.

1. Will you own a home in five years? (Check "yes" if you own a home now.)

Yes _____ No _____

If not, how many years will it be until you buy a home?

2. What do you expect your monthly mortgage to be?

3. **How much money will you have to put down on a house?**

How much for the closing costs and incidentals?

Do you have that money now?   Yes _____   No _____

4. **Are you currently in other debt?**

Yes _____   No _____

Do you have a plan to reduce or eliminate this debt?

How long will it take to reduce or eliminate this debt?

5. **How much time will you and your partner need for educational purposes to further your careers and improve your earning potential?**

	You	Partner
Five years	_____	_____
Ten years	_____	_____
Fifteen years	_____	_____

6. **What other big ticket items do you want to purchase (swimming pool, boat, camper, vacations)?** List the items and their estimated cost.

In five years

In ten years

In fifteen years

7. Which of the following would be nice to have for your child, if money could be found in your financial plan to cover the expense?

	Cost	Priority
Private preschool	_____	_____
Private elementary school	_____	_____
Private high school	_____	_____
College	_____	_____
Sports	_____	_____
Summer camp	_____	_____
Live-in nanny	_____	_____

8. Which of the following MUST you have for your child?

	Cost	Priority
Private preschool	_____	_____
Private elementary school	_____	_____
Private high school	_____	_____
College	_____	_____
Sports	_____	_____
Summer camp	_____	_____
Live-in nanny	_____	_____

9. How much would you like to have in savings for emergencies, disability, medical expenses, and other possible expenses?

In five years

In ten years

In fifteen years

Investments

THERE WAS A PROGRAM on television not so long ago about people who had won the lottery. All of the individuals who were profiled had won $10 million or more. They also had something else in common: they all were broke. Although many were scheduled to receive annual payments for years, they had either borrowed against the money or spent it already. Some of these people had even declared bankruptcy.

Before you start shaking your head in disgust, you might want to consider that many of us are making the same mistake. We all receive regular payments that amount to a potential fortune; in fact, you and your partner can accumulate millions of dollars during your working years. If you earn $25,000 a year at age twenty-five and work steadily until age sixty-five, without ever increasing your income, you'd have $1 million. It's up to you to spend and save all that money wisely so that you don't end up borrowing against or losing it.

Not all investments are created equal, of course. For example, although savings and checking accounts are easy to understand, they are frequently the least advantageous investments, as far as interest rates are concerned. As you move into other interest-bearing vehicles and more sophisticated investments, the level of complexity—and the level of risk—increases.

Before we discuss risks and investment options, it might be helpful to become familiar with the terms and jargon used in the industry.

Definitions

Annuity. A life insurer's contract providing tax-deferred earnings. Annuity income can be paid out over a lifetime or a set number of years. There are many types of annuities, but the two most common are the single premium annuity (SPA) and the deferred annuity. The SPA requires a single lump sum investment, while a deferred annuity requires monthly payments over a period of time. Annuities not only provide tax-deferred income, but they can serve as collateral for low-interest loans. Because the loan can be paid out of the death benefit, policy owners essentially get tax-free access to their earnings. The disadvantages of annuities include high, up-front commissions and surrender fees between 7 and 10 percent of the amount withdrawn if you cash out early in the contract. The government gets you for early withdrawal as well, charging a 10 percent penalty (in addition to normal taxes on income) if you withdraw before the age of fifty-nine-and-a-half.

Bonds. A bond allows you to loan money to someone—usually a business, government, or utility—for a specific length of time at a determined interest rate. Just as a bank pays you interest on your savings account, the entity to which you loan money (in the form of a bond) pays you interest. Bond interest is paid every six months. Bonds are rated according to the issuing company's ability to repay investors. They range from safe, investment-grade bonds to risky, high yield or junk bonds.

Certificates of deposit. Also called CDs, certificates of deposit are interest-bearing investments offered by banks. CDs can be purchased in increments of $100, with maturity ranging anywhere from a few weeks to several years. The interest rates offered on CDs vary. Usually, the longer the term, the higher the interest rate. The downside to CDs is that the investment is tied up for the entire term; you will pay a stiff penalty for cashing out early. Financial experts advise shopping around for the best interest rates on CDs. Some institutions offer as much as one full percentage point above the rates offered by local banks.

Diversification. Spreading out investments into many different investment vehicles to reduce the risk that one or more stocks or funds will perform badly.

Dollar cost averaging. The process of investing small amounts over a regular period of time. You buy multiple shares of a stock or fund, first at low rates, then at higher rates, thereby minimizing your risk.

Income tax deferral. On some investments, you still have to pay taxes, but not until sometime in the future.

Individual Retirement Account (IRA). A tax-deferred savings plan available to anyone with employment income. Contributions may be tax deductible (up to $2,000 a year for an individual and $4,000 for a couple), depending on your income and whether you or your spouse are covered by a pension. There is a 10 percent penalty for early withdrawal before the age of fifty-nine-and-a-half. See also *Roth IRA*.

Laddering. Buying different investments that have different lengths of time until maturity to avoid having all of your investments mature at once.

Liquidity. The ability to cash in investments quickly to obtain their cash value.

Load. The fee charged on a mutual fund to pay for professional management. Loads can be as much as 5 percent, although the standard fee is between 1 and 2 percent. Some funds charge loads for buying, some for selling, and some for buying and selling. A no-load fund does not charge for these services.

Municipal bonds. Sometimes called a muni, a municipal bond is issued by a municipality, or city. Interest paid on a municipal bond is generally tax free; because of this, the interest rate is usually lower than it would be for a taxable bond. You can take your money out of munis at any time without paying a tax penalty.

Mutual funds. A mutual fund is a group of stocks, bonds, and securities that are purchased and treated as a single investment. As the value of the investments within the fund increases, the value of the mutual fund increases; of course, as is the case with any investment tied to stocks, if the value of the investments within the fund decreases, the value of the mutual fund also decreases. Each fund's specific objectives and guidelines are detailed in the company's prospectus. Mutual funds are managed by professionals in the investment industry who choose each stock or bond for its potential and monitor the performance of each carefully. Investors can screen mutual funds according to any number of criteria, including friendliness to the environment, social responsibility, labor policies, or financial performance alone.

Roth IRA. Type of IRA where contributions are made after taxes, but income is tax-free. Once you put your money in, you never pay taxes on it again. Withdrawals are not reportable income and won't affect your adjusted gross income during retirement. Individuals with a gross income less than $110,000 and married couples with a combined gross income of less than $160,000 are eligible for this fund.

Savings and checking accounts. There are several kinds of checking and savings accounts.

- **Savings accounts.** Passbook savings and standard savings accounts allow people to keep their money safe while earning interest at a nominal rate.
- **Money market accounts.** A money market account is similar to a savings account, but interest rates are based on the U.S. Treasury auction discount rates.
- **No-fee checking accounts.** Most banks, particularly credit unions, offer some sort of no-fee checking account. Charges for check processing are waived, so the only expense involved, if any, is the cost of printing the checks. Credit unions will often pay interest on these accounts, although the rate is low.
- **NOW accounts.** A NOW account is a no-fee checking account that requires a minimum daily balance. By maintaining that balance, you get free checking plus interest. If your balance falls below the minimum, you still earn interest but pay a service charge.
- **Investment accounts.** An investment account is a checking account that requires a larger daily balance than a NOW account, but does not charge a service fee. Interest is based on market conditions. If you fall below the minimum balance, your interest rate drops to that of a NOW account until your balance reaches the minimum balance amount.

Series EE bonds. The Series EE savings bond is a security that accrues interest until it is cashed or reaches final maturity in thirty years. There are eight denominations: $50, $75, $100, $200, $500, $1,000, $5,000, and $10,000. The purchase price of an EE bond is one-half of the denomination; for example, you can purchase a $50 bond for $25. Series EE bonds continue to increase in value as long as you hold them for up to 30 years. These increases in value aren't limited by the face amount of the bond. So, depending on interest rates and how long you keep your bond, its value can be greater than its face amount.

Stocks. A stock is an equity investment that represents a piece, or a share, of a company. *Common stock* is normal ownership in a company; preferred stock is stock with a claim on the company's earnings before payment can be made on common stock, should the company liquidate or declare a dividend. *Blue chip stocks* are those with a long history (twenty-five years or more) of stable value and consistent dividend payments. *Growth stocks* are those that increase in share price as the company's market value increases. The value of shares goes up and down, which affects the amount of money you make or lose if you sell. If you buy stock and sell it after its value has increased, you make money; if you buy stock and sell it when the value has dropped, you lose money.

Tax-qualified retirement plan. A tax-favored employee benefit plan will defer taxation on both contributions and earnings until the money is withdrawn, usually at retirement age. Includes 401(k), 403(b), and Keogh (for people with self-employment income). Most companies deduct contributions from employee paychecks (and sometimes match them), then offer employees several choices about how and where they'd like to invest, including mutual funds, separate growth stocks, and even the company's own stock.

Treasury Bills. Also called T-bills, Treasury Bills cost $10,000, and mature in either ninety days, one hundred eighty days, or one year. You can buy T-bills from a broker for a fee, or order them by mail from a Federal Reserve Bank without paying a fee (ask your bank for the address of the nearest Federal Reserve Bank).

Treasury Bonds. A Treasury Bond is nothing more than a bond issued by the federal government and backed by the U.S. Treasury. Treasury Bonds are usually held for seven years or more, and interest earned on them is not subject to state income tax.

Treasury Notes. Treasury Notes have maturity dates of up to ten years. They are sold in two- and three-year denominations for $5,000, and in four- to ten-year denominations for $1,000.

Zero coupon bonds. Government bonds that don't accumulate interest, but pay off in a single lump sum upon maturity.

Risk

MOST PEOPLE THINK that the loss of principal is the only risk they face when they invest. They worry that if they invest $10,000 in stocks today, they might end up with only $9,000 tomorrow. What they don't consider is that there are many other risks, as well—risks tied to reinvestment, inflation, and taxation. Even interest rates present a risk. For instance, if you buy a five-year CD at 6 percent interest, and a year later, the interest rate for a five-year CD jumps to 8 percent, you lose; your money is still tied up for four more years at a lower rate.

You can't avoid risk, no matter where you invest your money. However, different types of investments will have different levels of risk. For instance, if your priority is to hold on to your principal, you might put your money into a CD at a bank or credit union that is insured by the FDIC. This means that even if the bank or credit union goes bankrupt, the federal government will cover your principal up to $100,000, so you would not lose your money.

On the other hand, you might invest $100,000 in a start-up company's stock. There is no way to know for sure that the company will wow the market and be a smashing success; it could just as easily be out of business in a year, and you could lose the entire amount. Because the potential for success is lower, there has to be a higher promise of return to entice investors. A start-up company has a high risk factor, but the return, should it pan out, could be fairly high as well.

What does all of this mean to you?

You want all of your investments to go up, up, up in value. The reality of the market is that rates of return fluctuate wildly, depending on the type of investment, its level of risk, what's going on in the market, taxes, inflation, and when you cash out. Your financial future will depend on the levels of risk you choose, and how well those choices pan out. If you have forty years left before retirement, you might be willing to take on more risk, since you could still recover from losses; if you are retiring in five years and must be sure the money you need will be there, you might choose less risky options.

The important thing is to choose a level of risk you can live with. To use a stress-level metaphor, you'll probably want to choose something that lies between white-water rafting and nodding off in the easy chair.

In almost every case, it's best to diversify your risk by spreading your investment between high-, medium-, and low-risk investments. If you want to play in the high-risk category, keep a small amount in reserve to play with.

Investing in stocks is meant for those who know what they're doing, but anyone can participate in the stock market through a professionally managed mutual fund. Let the experts make money for you.

Taxes

SHORTLY AFTER NICK was born, I invested in stocks for the first time. I had been following a start-up company with some very exciting products, and I bought a few shares when the stock was under $2. Although I'd planned to keep the stock for years and invest it for Nick, it began to rise. I sold it two months later for about $12 a share.

Well, Wizard of Wall Street that I was, I kept the money in an account with my broker and continued to buy and sell stock. They all performed well.

A year went by, and I was introduced to an unpleasant fact of life called *capital gains tax*. I had been naive enough to assume that because the money I had made stayed in my account, I wouldn't be taxed on it until I cashed it in.

Wrong. All the gains that I had made through that year were taxed as income.

The moral of the story is this: you must consider the tax implications of buying and selling stocks. When will you be taxed on a transaction? Is it possible to offset a potential gain with losses in other areas? Discuss your investment plans with your accountant or tax preparer to know for sure.

Financial Planning

IT IS AT THIS POINT that some people become completely overwhelmed. They may not feel able to develop a comprehensive financial plan, because they don't believe they have a grasp of savings and investment options. If this sounds like you, don't despair. Your work has not been in vain! Take the worksheets you've completed on the previous pages to a professional financial planner. He or she can help you develop a well-balanced financial plan that you can live with.

Even if you will be meeting with a financial planner, however, you may want to think about the questions in the following section. This is a typical worksheet that a financial planner may use when working with you. Use it as a tool to discuss investment ideas with your partner. It will help you clarify your thinking about the types of investments you prefer.

Investment Information

1. How would you describe your investment philosophy?

Very Conservative	_____
Conservative	_____
Income-Oriented	_____
Balanced (Growth and Income)	_____
Growth	_____
Aggressive Growth	_____
Other	_____

If you selected "other," please describe in a few words:

2. Prioritize your financial goals.

Goals	Need By	Priority
Down payment—new home	_____	_____
Down payment—second home	_____	_____
Vehicle purchase	_____	_____
Wedding	_____	_____
College tuition (yours)	_____	_____
College tuition (partner's)	_____	_____
College tuition (child's)	_____	_____
Care for aging parents	_____	_____
Retirement	_____	_____
Other	_____	_____
Other	_____	_____
Other	_____	_____
Other	_____	_____

3. What is your current tax bracket?

4. **What is your partner's annual income?**

   How stable is this income?
   Very _____ Average _____ Somewhat _____ Unstable _____

5. **What is your annual income?**

   How stable is this income?
   Very _____ Average _____ Somewhat _____ Unstable _____

6. **What type of life insurance coverage do you have?**

7. **Do you have disability insurance?**

8. **Which of your current holdings would you like an opinion on?**

Annuities	_____
IRA/401k	_____
Mutual Funds	_____
Stocks	_____
Bonds	_____
Savings	_____
Partnerships	_____
Other	_____

Investing for Your Child's College Education

YOU ALREADY KNOW that you'll need $334,000 to raise your child. You also have eighteen years to save for the ever-rising costs of tuition, room and board, books, and other college expenses.

Parents have different philosophies about their role in providing a child's education. Some parents see it as their responsibility—just another part of the parenting contract. Others wish to pay only a portion of the expense, theorizing that the child will appreciate the education more if he or she assumes at least part of the responsibility.

According to the Spring 1998 issue of the *T. Rowe Price Report,* children attending college in the year 2016 would need an estimated $104,000 for a four-year program at a public college or a $222,000 for a four-year program at a private university. This includes tuition, room and board, transportation, books, and other expenses, and assumes a 5 percent annual cost increase. This means that with an annual investment return of 8 percent, parents would have to invest about $220 a month for a public education, or $460 a month for a private education.

There are as many college fund strategies as there are colleges. The following tactic is known as "pyramiding" your risk. It's an example of how you could assume a high level of risk when the child is a baby, then decrease your risk as the college years approach.

- **Fifteen to twenty years before college.** Focus most of your portfolio on growth stock mutual funds. Set up automatic investments every month and spread the money among several funds:

  60% Capital stock funds

  15% International stocks

  10% Long-term bonds

  10% Intermediate-term bonds

  5% Cash equivalent

- **Ten to fifteen years before college.** It might be time to lighten up on the amount of risk. Try:

  65% U.S. growth stock funds

  15% International funds

  10% Bond funds/fixed income

  10% CDs

- **Five to ten years before college.** Begin to move 15% or so of your investments into more conservative holdings.

    40% Low-risk equities

    60% U.S. Treasuries

- **Two years before college.** Start cashing in stock funds. Move half of the investments to CDs and intermediate-term bonds. Just before college starts, move two years' worth of cash over to a money market fund so you can write checks against it. Keep the remainder in fairly short-term investments that you can cash out as needed.

Crib Notes

Tip #26. Do what you love and the money will follow.

If your dream is to own your own bowling alley, go for it. If you love it, if it makes you happy, the money will come. Also, you'll be a better father, husband, and person if you are doing what makes you happy.

Tip #27. Put money in child's name.

Often there is a tax advantage by setting up a UGMA (Universal Gift to Minors Act) or UTMA (Uniform Transfer to Minors Act) account.

Tip #28. When investing, remember 72.

Here's the formula for calculating how long it will take you to double your investment: 72 divided by the interest rate. For example, if you have a fund with a 5 percent interest rate, 72 divided by 5 equals 14. It will take you fourteen years to double your money.

Tip #29. Make a will.

Even if you do not have many assets, prepare a will to establish guardianship for your child. In some states, if both parents die and there is no will, the children are placed in foster care.

Resources

Books

Bangs, David H. *The Business Planning Guide: Creating A Plan for Success in Your Own Business.* Chicago: Dearborn Trade, 1996.

Godfrey, Neale S., and Tad Richards. *From Cradle to College.* New York: Harper Business, 1997.

Kobliner, Beth. *Get A Financial Life: Personal Finance in Your Twenties and Thirties.* New York: Simon & Schuster, 1995.

Malkiel, Burton G. *A Random Walk Down Wall Street.* New York: W.W. Norton & Co., 1996.

Orman, Suze, and Linda Mead. *You've Earned It, Don't Lose It: Mistakes You Can't Afford to Make When You Retire.* New York: Newmarket Press, 1997.

Organizations

National Association of Securities Dealers (NASD)
Consumer Arbitration Center
33 Whitehall St.
New York, NY 10004
Phone (212) 858-4000
The NASD primarily handles disputes between customers and brokers, but also distributes a number of financial publications.

For a list of certified financial planners in your area, call the Institute of Certified Financial Planners at 1-800-282-7526.

✒ BUYING A HOME ✒

Ahh. Someday Abu, things are going to change. We'll be rich. Live in a
palace. And never have any problems at all.
—Aladdin

On the night Nick was born, I came home to our little apartment and sat in the dark, thinking of all the things I had to do. I had to learn how to throw a curve ball, or at least learn what a curve ball was so I could fake it. I had to read more, so I could answer questions like, why doesn't an igloo melt? Most of all, we had to get a house.

Before Nick came along, it wasn't important to own a home. For one thing, we weren't sure if we would be staying in the area, and we didn't want to be tied down if we decided to move. We also liked certain aspects of the renter-landlord relationship. Something broken? Call the landlord. Don't like the way something looks? Call the landlord. Want to be sure you can hear the television on hot, sticky summer days? Ask the landlord to mow during commercials, or at least to not pass out from heat exhaustion until he gets to the far side of the building (those paramedics can be so noisy).

But after Nick was born, we realized that we had probably paid enough in rent over the years to have purchased a small mansion and three summer homes. It was time to buy our own place.

Finding a Realtor

SOME PEOPLE STRIKE OUT alone in their quest for a house, but most contact a Realtor for help. Realtors undergo rigorous testing before they get their licenses, and believe me, there are reasons for it. Without knowing what to look for, you can end up involved in all kinds of nasty legal situations. It's wise to find a Realtor, especially when you're about to buy your first home.

You might think that the Realtor works for you, the buyer, and that his or her only role is to guide and protect you through the confusing and difficult process of buying a home. In most cases, however, the Realtor actually works for the seller. He or she is motivated to sell you a piece of property, not to help you find the perfect home, and will receive a commission when the house sells. Of course, there are Realtors who will do their best to make sure you get what you're looking for. Shop around; find one who is flexible and easy to work with, one who has a good understanding of what you are looking for. Personal recommendations and word of mouth are often the best way to find a good Realtor.

Once you decide to work with someone, ask for his or her advice and get explanations for things that seem unclear or confusing. Buying a home—any type of home—can be complicated. There is a good deal to know and a lot of information coming at you all at once. A good Realtor will help you sort through it.

First-Time Home Buyer Programs

MANY CITIES AND COUNTIES offer special financing to first-time home buyers who qualify. To see what is available, contact your city or township office, either where you live currently or where you're planning to buy a home. Sometimes, grants are given to cover closing costs; other times, cities broker lending services and can negotiate a lower interest rate.

In addition to financial services and money-saving programs, most cities offer special classes or seminars on purchasing a home. Community education classes, which are typically taught by professionals in the real estate industry, cover such topics as budgeting, finding a Realtor, qualifying for a mortgage, hiring an inspector, asking the right questions, negotiating with sellers, putting in a bid, and speaking the jargon. In communities where special financing and grants are available, classes can alert students to what's out there and how to find it. It is worth the time to spend a few evenings or a weekend in classes like these. The information offered is valuable and practical, and could save you a bundle.

Housing Options

NOT EVERYONE WANTS to live in a small house with a white picket fence, an apple tree in the backyard, and a tire swing. When it comes to buying your first home, there are many different options.

Mobile Homes

For many couples, particularly those who are just starting out, mobile homes may offer the most sensible option. They're not as expensive as houses, so the monthly payments are less. In fact, some used models sell for only a few thousand dollars.

One of the main deterrents to buying a mobile home is that it depreciates quickly, like a car. However, if you buy a used mobile home and keep it in good condition, you can generally get out of it what you paid for it.

Size can be another deterrent, but you may be surprised. Many mobile homes, especially modular units and double-wides, have the look and feel of a rather large apartment. Modulars and double-wides don't depreciate as rapidly as other types of mobile homes, but they don't increase in value like conventional homes, either.

When buying a mobile home, there are certain questions you should ask yourself.

- **Where will you put it?** Will you buy a piece of property and put the mobile home on it? If so, make sure the land is zoned for mobile-home living. You will need to budget for land costs and monthly taxes on that land, as well as the expense of transporting the mobile home to the location and installing heat, water, and electricity.

- **Does the area need to be cleared or landscaped? Does a driveway need to be poured?**
- **Are there any fees to consider?** If you're going to live in a trailer park, you will be paying park or association fees. Sometimes, these fees are so high that it doesn't make sense to live there.

Condominiums

Often called condos, these are essentially apartments that you own. In addition to the mortgage payment, you will pay maintenance fees for such services as snow removal, lawn care, and other building maintenance. If you're not particularly handy or do not have a green thumb, living in a condo offers the advantage of having all of those internal and external chores taken care of for you.

The housing market for condos tends to fluctuate more widely than the market for traditional homes. Sometimes, the bottom falls out of the market; at other times, condos are in demand. You may be able to get a terrific deal on a condo, but be prepared: selling can be difficult.

Duplexes

Duplexes, or doubles, can be a wonderful option, particularly if you want help with the mortgage payment. If you own both parts of a duplex, you can live in half of it and rent out the other half. In many cases, the rent you receive will pay for most, if not all, of the mortgage. If you pay off the mortgage early, the rent money becomes extra income. Another option is to rent out both halves of the duplex and use the extra rental income to buy a new house.

Before purchasing a duplex, consider the problems of owning rental property: not finding tenants, having irresponsible tenants who do not take care of the house, experiencing a lack of privacy, and being responsible for the maintenance and repair of a two-family home.

Townhouses

Townhouses are similar to condos, in terms of the pros and cons of the investment. Like condos, there is a monthly charge for such services as lawn care, snow removal, and general upkeep. The market value of townhouses, however, can fluctuate dramatically. When compared to condos, townhouses typically have higher market values, more privacy and space, and sometimes even a lawn and deck area. Many families live in townhouses. If you do consider buying a townhouse, get to know your neighbors on both sides. You will be sharing a wall with both of them, so it is important that your lifestyles be compatible. Better yet, get an end unit; that way, you'll only have to share one wall.

Co-ops

Co-ops are similar to condos, except the residents own shares in a corporation that owns the building. Each co-op sets its own rules for the building, and the residents are voting members. There are typically monthly fees, called "association fees" or "co-op dues," for maintaining the building and grounds.

There are some obvious disadvantages. For one thing, the co-op could vote to require all homes to be white with black shutters, in which case you can forget your idea about living in a blue house with with a red door. Also, like any corporation, a co-op is subject to certain risks; it can sell to another company or declare bankruptcy.

Traditional Homes

The most popular housing alternative is the two- or three-bedroom house with a couple of shade trees and a nice big backyard. The main advantage to owning this type of home is it will almost always increase in value, although researching property values beforehand and checking out the adjoining areas are always wise. Another advantage: it's easy to expand or remodel a traditional home. If you need additional space at some point in the future, you can often convert basements and attics into bedrooms, offices, or dens. Finally, there is more privacy in a traditional house; when you don't share a common wall with another family, you do not have to listen to their television set or vacuum cleaner.

The primary disadvantage to owning a traditional home is that you are responsible for all maintenance and repairs: all the lawn mowing, leaf raking, snow shoveling, furnace fixing, pavement sealing, driveway tarring, and shingle laying, to name a few. And if you don't do it yourself, you'll have to pay someone else to do it for you. Taxes are another disadvantage. Single-family homes carry a large percentage of the tax burden in many communities; the newer the community, the higher those taxes are likely to be.

Once you know what type of housing will work best for you, the next step is to decide what features you and your partner will want to have in your new home. Each of you should go through the following list of features. Give one point to each feature that you feel is important. Have your partner do the same. The features that score two points should become part of your search criteria.

Your Dream House

How Important Is . . .	For Him	For Her	Total
Den	_____	_____	_____
Office	_____	_____	_____
Guest room	_____	_____	_____
Family room	_____	_____	_____
Room for each child	_____	_____	_____
Laundry room	_____	_____	_____
Mud room	_____	_____	_____
Workshop	_____	_____	_____
Garage	_____	_____	_____
School system	_____	_____	_____
A short commute:			
for you	_____	_____	_____
for your partner	_____	_____	_____
Living near:			
your family	_____	_____	_____
your partner's family	_____	_____	_____
a playground	_____	_____	_____
Other	_____	_____	_____
Other	_____	_____	_____
Other	_____	_____	_____

When to Buy

MANY EXPERTS CLAIM that there is a right time of year to buy a home. Fewer homes are sold in late December and during the holidays than at any other time of the year. Owners who must sell during this time are usually desperate, especially if their home has been on the market all year, and they will often do whatever it takes to sell. The seller's desperation works to the buyer's advantage.

The worst time of year to buy, according to experts, is in late spring and early summer. This is peak real estate season. Most buyers start looking for a home in the spring, and those with families will want to move while the weather is nice and their children are out of school. Although the selection is good at this time of year, competition for bargains is high, and owners aren't usually as willing to negotiate.

The right time to buy isn't just determined by the calendar, however. The following factors are crucial when assessing whether or not you are ready to buy a house.

You should buy your first home . . .

1. When you can afford it. After you have fine-tuned your budget, delete your rent payment and insert your mortgage payment. Include principal, interest, insurance, and property taxes, plus 10 percent for emergencies (and there will be plenty of emergencies, believe me). If your budget doesn't squeal, choke, and hiss, that's a good sign.

2. When you can afford all of the down payment and closing costs yourself, or can borrow from your family and friends and pay them back within a year or so. If you borrow the money, add the amount you will pay back each month into your budget and see if it still works. Even if the lender is dear old Mom, budgeting to pay this money back is important. You will have a sense of fulfillment when you make the last payment.

3. When the money you have, or are borrowing, can cover everything. Besides the down payment and closing costs, other expenses are sure to arise. Will the house need to be painted in the first year? Will you need a lawn mower, snow shovels, or lawn rakes? Do you need appliances or furniture? You should not plan to trash existing, working appliances just because you think it would be really neat to have a brand new purple washer, dryer, and forty-five cubic foot refrigerator with an ice maker and water dispenser. But don't plan to sleep on the floor and wash your clothes in the sink for the first year, either.

4. When you're buying for the right reasons. There are many good reasons to buy a home. You may want a place where you can raise a family, or you might want to start building equity, for instance. But don't buy just because all the other couples you know are buying houses, because you want to crank your stereo up without people complaining, or because you don't want to admit that you're still renting when your class reunion rolls around.

5. When your instincts about the house, trailer, condo, or igloo are good. You can do mental computations and run the "what ifs" forever, but there's one additional thing you need to check: your gut. Again, don't ignore what your instincts are telling you. They'll never let you down.

Pre-Qualifying

BEING PRE-QUALIFIED IS somewhat of a misnomer. It does not mean that you have already been approved for a mortgage. Pre-qualifying helps you determine the price of a house that you would be qualified to buy. However, be aware that the price range estimate may be at the extreme high end of what you can comfortably afford. In other words, you may be pre-qualified for a $250,000 house, but the mortgage payments might stretch your budget to the absolute limit. You will sleep much easier at night if you buy a house well below that amount.

The following worksheet will help you gain a more accurate view of what you can afford in a mortgage payment. Compare that figure to the pre-qualified amount, and choose a realistic amount in between.

1. Calculate your adjusted gross monthly income.

Your yearly gross income: $ _____

1. Divide your yearly gross income by 12.
      Monthly gross income: $ _____

2. Multiply your monthly gross income by .64.
      Adjusted gross monthly income: $ _____ (A)

2. Calculate your monthly expenses.

Food $ _____
Medical insurance $ _____
Medical bills not covered by insurance $ _____
Car insurance $ _____
Car loans $ _____
Gasoline $ _____
Other transportation $ _____
Credit cards $ _____
Other loans $ _____
Child care $ _____
Alimony or child support $ _____
Clothing $ _____
Charity $ _____
Entertainment $ _____
Dues and subscriptions $ _____
Other_____ $ _____

                  Total monthly expenses: $ _____ (B)

3. Calculate your maximum monthly house payment.

1. Subtract your total monthly expenses (B) from your adjusted gross monthly income (A): $ _____

2. Multiply the amount above by .9 to allow for emergency expenditures. (If you want to be more conservative, multiply by .85 or .8). This is your maximum monthly house payment:

$ _____ (C)

4. Adjust for taxes and insurance to calculate the principal and interest of the maximum monthly house payment.

1. Contact your Realtor for an estimate of the monthly property taxes in your area. $ _____

2. Contact an insurance agent to obtain a monthly estimate of the homeowners' insurance premium. $ _____

3. Add these together (estimate for property taxes plus homeowner's insurance premium): $ _____ (D)

5. Subtract (D) from (C): $ _____

This is your maximum monthly principal and interest.

Once you have determined the maximum monthly principal and interest you can afford, use the grids on pages 149 and 150 to see what kind of a mortgage you can apply for. Match the monthly payment with an interest rate you think you can get, and you'll be able to estimate your monthly mortgage payment.

Even though a mortgage company may approve you for a specific monthly mortgage, it is not necessarily the right amount for you. You can often get approved for a fairly wide range—say, somewhere between $68,000 and $79,000. Remember, this looks better on paper than it will in the real world. If you think you can just barely swing that monthly mortgage payment, you may be spending too much.

Although mortgage companies make an enormous amount of money from the interest rate on your mortgage over the years, they will not lose if they foreclose on your home. These companies don't want to wipe you out financially, but they do expect to make a profit, so they have built certain safeguards into the system to make sure they get what's coming to them.

Typically, mortgage companies go on the 30 percent rule: your debt payments, including your mortgage, insurance, and taxes, total 30 percent of your income. On a conventional mortgage, when your down payment is less than 20 percent, lenders usually charge you a higher interest rate and require you to purchase private mortgage insurance to protect them from losses if you default on your loan. This insurance is added to your monthly rate. When you have built up 20 percent equity, your mortgage payment goes down. FHA-insured and VA-guaranteed loans also protect lenders against possible borrower default by attaching additional mortgage insurance to monthly payments.

Sometimes materialism corrupts good sense, and instead of a cute little starter home, you go for the four-bedroom colonial. Next thing you know, you have a huge mortgage payment, your taxes are twice what they would have been on a smaller house, and if you add in a few of the basics, like a stove, refrigerator, washer, and dryer, you have used up all available credit on your credit cards. And you don't even have any furniture yet. Think about your financial goals before rushing headlong into a mortgage you cannot afford. Concentrate on the long term; look at the larger picture.

In addition to interest rates, you need to consider the length of the mortgage. A fifteen-year mortgage for a $100,000 house will cost $69,430.40 in interest, but interest on a thirty-year mortgage for that same house will be $157,907.60. If you choose the higher monthly payments for a fifteen-year mortgage, you would save $88,477.20 on your home.

Thirty-Year Mortgage

Monthly Payment	6%	6.5%	7%	7.5%	8%	8.5%	9%	9.5%	10%	10.5%	11%	12%	13%
$300	50,037	47,463	45,092	42,905	40,885	39,016	37,285	35,678	34,185	32,796	31,502	29,166	27,120
$400	66,717	63,284	60,123	57,207	54,513	52,021	49,713	47,571	45,580	43,728	42,003	38,887	36,160
$500	83,396	79,105	75,154	71,519	68,142	65,027	62,141	59,463	56,975	54,660	52,503	48,609	45,200
$600	100,075	94,926	90,185	85,811	81,770	78,032	74,569	71,356	68,370	65,592	63,004	58,331	54,240
$700	116,754	110,748	105,215	100,112	95,398	91,038	86,997	83,249	79,766	76,525	73,504	68,053	63,280
$800	133,433	126,569	120,246	114,414	109,027	104,043	99,425	95,141	91,161	87,457	84,005	77,775	72,320
$900	150,112	142,390	135,277	128,716	122,655	117,048	111,854	107,034	102,556	98,389	94,506	87,497	81,360
$1000	166,792	158,211	150,308	143,018	136,283	130,054	124,282	118,927	113,951	109,321	105,006	97,218	90,400
$1100	183,471	174,032	165,338	157,319	149,912	143,059	136,710	130,819	125,346	120,253	115,507	106,940	99,440
$1200	200,150	189,853	180,368	171,621	163,540	156,064	149,138	142,712	136,741	131,185	126,008	116,662	108,480
$1300	216,829	205,674	195,400	185,923	177,169	169,070	161,566	154,605	148,136	142,117	136,508	126,384	117,519
$1400	233,508	221,495	210,431	200,225	190,797	182,075	173,995	166,497	159,531	153,049	147,009	136,106	126,559
$1500	250,187	237,316	225,461	214,526	204,425	195,080	186,423	178,390	170,926	163,981	157,510	145,828	135,599
$1600	266,867	253,137	240,482	228,828	218,054	208,086	198,851	190,283	182,321	174,913	168,010	155,549	144,539
$1700	283,546	268,958	255,523	243,130	231,682	221,091	211,279	202,175	193,716	185,845	178,511	165,271	153,671
$1800	300,225	284,779	270,554	257,432	245,310	234,097	223,707	214,068	205,111	196,777	189,011	174,993	162,719

Fifteen-Year Mortgage

Monthly Payment	6%	6.5%	7%	7.5%	8%	8.5%	9%	9.5%	10%	10.5%	11%	12%	13%
$300	35,551	34,439	33,377	32,362	31,392	30,465	29,578	28,729	27,917	27,140	26,395	24,997	23,711
$400	47,401	45,919	44,502	43,149	41,856	40,620	39,437	38,306	37,223	36,186	35,193	33,329	31,615
$500	59,252	57,398	55,628	53,937	52,320	50,775	49,297	47,882	46,529	45,223	43,991	41,661	39,518
$600	71,102	68,878	66,754	64,724	62,784	60,930	59,156	57,459	55,834	54,279	52,789	49,993	47,422
$700	82,952	80,357	77,879	75,511	73,248	71,085	69,015	67,035	65,140	63,326	61,587	58,325	55,325
$800	94,803	91,837	89,005	86,299	83,712	81,240	78,875	76,612	74,446	72,732	70,386	66,657	63,229
$900	106,653	103,317	100,130	97,086	94,177	91,395	88,734	86,118	83,752	81,419	79,184	74,990	71,133
$1000	118,504	114,796	111,256	107,873	104,641	101,550	98,593	95,765	93,057	90,465	87,982	83,322	79,036
$1100	130,354	126,276	122,382	118,661	115,105	111,705	108,453	105,341	102,363	99,512	96,780	91,654	86,940
$1200	142,204	137,756	133,507	129,448	125,569	121,860	118,312	114,918	111,669	108,558	105,578	99,986	94,844
$1300	154,055	149,235	144,633	140,235	136,033	132,015	128,171	124,494	120,975	117,605	114,377	106,318	102,747
$1400	165,905	160,715	155,758	151,023	146,497	142,170	138,031	134,071	130,280	126,651	123,175	116,650	110,651
$1500	177,755	172,195	166,884	161,810	156,961	152,325	147,890	143,647	139,586	135,698	131,973	124,983	118,554
$1600	189,606	183,674	178,010	172,597	167,425	162,480	157,749	153,224	148,892	144,744	140,771	133,315	126,458
$1700	201,456	195,154	189,135	183,385	177,889	172,634	167,609	162,800	158,198	153,791	149,569	141,647	134,362
$1800	213,306	206,634	200,261	194,172	188,353	182,789	177,468	172,377	167,503	162,837	158,367	149,979	142,265

Glossary of Mortgage Terms

Adjustable-rate mortgage. See *variable-rate mortgage.*

Amortization. The gradual reduction of a loan over time.

Amortization schedule. The schedule that breaks down the life of the loan by each payment made, showing interest and principal paid and the remaining balance.

Balloon loan. A loan where the last payment is considerably larger than all the payments before.

Closing. The process in which the ownership of a piece of property is transferred.

Closing costs. Fees and expenses incurred in the purchase of property. Costs include points, lawyer's fees, title search, escrow payments, origination fees, Realtor's commissions, and so on. Commissions are usually paid by the seller. Closing costs do not include other costs paid at the time of closing (the down payment, for example). Typically, total closing costs average 3 to 5 percent of the mortgage value. Of course, this will vary from state to state and from lender to lender. (In some cases, particularly when the seller is anxious or desperate to sell the house, you can ask the seller to pay for part or all of the closing costs. Ask your lender or Realtor for details.)

Conventional mortgage. Type of mortgage where the buyer puts down 20 percent or more of the purchase price and is responsible for all property taxes and insurance.

Debt-to-income ratio. Ratio of monthly gross income as compared to monthly debt. Lenders use this formula to determine the amount for which a borrower can qualify.

Deed. Written document used to transfer a title.

Down payment. Partial payment needed when purchasing a home. It usually represents a percentage of the total cost, between 5 and 20 percent, but in some cases, properties can be purchased with little or no down payment.

Earnest money. Deposit put down on the property in good faith, in advance of the down payment.

Escrow. A borrower gives a deed and/or money to an independent entity to hold until certain conditions of a contract are met. Also, lenders of FHA mortgages hold in escrow the property taxes that are included in the monthly mortgage payment; the lender pays the taxes twice a year.

Fannie Mae. Federal National Mortgage Association. A private corporation that assists low- and middle-income families by acquiring government-assured mortgages through the FHA.

FHA. Federal Housing Administration. A division of the Department of Housing and Urban Development that provides financing to those who have little cash or a low income.

FHA mortgage. Mortgage where the FHA assumes the risk to the lender of nonpayment of mortgage. Both borrower and property must meet certain requirements.

Fixed-rate mortgage. Loan with a set rate of interest for the life of the mortgage.

FmHA. Farmers Home Administration. Federal agency that provides financing to low-income families in rural areas.

FSBO. For Sale By Owner. The owner of a property seeks a buyer without the aid of a Realtor.

Full disclosure. A requirement for real estate brokers to present all known information about a property to prospective buyers, or for a lender to disclose to borrowers the most effective cost and terms of loans.

GPM. Graduated payment mortgage. Monthly payments are less in the beginning of the loan and greater toward maturity.

Hazard insurance. Lenders require borrowers to have this insurance to protect the value of the house against such things as fires, storms, and water damage. Special flood insurance can also be purchased if the home is in a flood zone.

Homestead. State subsidy to reduce property taxes for primary residences. Homesteaded property taxes can be as much as 40 percent less than non-homesteaded property taxes.

Inspection. Examination of the interior, exterior, and surrounding property of a house to determine its condition and to ensure that building codes have been met.

Lock in. Buyers can lock in at a certain interest rate before the actual closing date, usually for a term of thirty, sixty, or ninety days. Locking in can be an advantage if interest rates are rising, but if they drop, buyers must pay the higher rate.

Mortgage insurance. Lenders require homeowners to have this type of insurance, whether private mortgage insurance on a conventional loan, or FHA insurance on an FHA loan, to protect against default. In either case, this insurance is required until the buyers have built up a 20 percent equity on the value of the loan.

Origination fee. Lenders charge this fee for paperwork, staff time, and other resources used to process loan applications. The fee is usually about 1 percent of the mortgage value.

Owner financing. Also called a *land contract,* owner financing is when the seller acts as the bank. You agree on a set interest rate and pay the seller monthly payments with interest until the home is paid for. This type of financing is used when a buyer would have difficulty getting a traditional mortgage. Usually requires a larger down payment.

Points. Considered prepaid interest, a point is a certain percentage of the selling price that buyers can pay the lender to reduce the interest rate on the mortgage. Each point represents 1 percent of the mortgage amount, and can buy down the interest rate by .25 percent.

Pre-approval. Approval for a certain amount of money a lender will loan. Pre-approval can help in the purchasing process, because buyers know up front how much they can borrow and sellers are more apt to accept a bid from buyers who have been pre-approved. Many banks offer pre-approval over the phone; after answering a few questions about income and debt, buyers are given a price range they will probably be approved for.

Prepayment. Buyers have the right to prepay the principal on a mortgage without penalty.

Principal. Amount of actual mortgage value, aside from interest. Though monthly payments remain constant over the life of a loan, amounts being applied toward interest and principal vary. See *amortization schedule.*

Purchase agreement. Written document stating the buyer's intention to purchase property.

Recision notice. Notice explaining the buyer's right to cancel the transaction. Federal law requires that buyers be given three days to rescind without cost to them.

Refinance. Repurchasing the property for a lower interest rate. Origination fees and closing costs may apply, so the interest rate must be low enough that refinancing is cost effective. Homeowners refinance to lower their monthly payments or shorten the life of their loan.

Rent with option to buy. Developed primarily for those who have difficulty coming up with a down payment, renting with the option to buy works like this: the buyer agrees to rent property for a certain period of time, usually one year, after which time he or she has the option to buy the property and have a percentage of the rent paid go toward the purchase price. There are no set rules for this type of plan, so beware. Inspect the property before you rent, and then draw up a contract listing all terms, the percentage of rent paid that will apply toward purchase price, who will be responsible for repairs and upkeep during the rental, what is included with purchase (curtains, carpet, appliances, and so forth), and who will finance the mortgage. Be sure to negotiate the best deal on a purchase price and the percentage of rent going toward that purchase. Have a lawyer look over the contract before you sign.

Survey. Accurate measurement of land to determine the property's borders. Often required by lenders as part of the mortgage process.

Title. Physical document that proves ownership of a piece of property.

Title search. Buyers can pay to have the title history investigated for improper procedures, fraud, forgery, unresolved ownership, liens against property, assessments, and zone violations.

Torrens. State-sponsored system of registration for land titles. Not applicable in all states.

Variable-rate mortgage. Sometimes abbreviated VRM, variable-rate mortgages fluctuate from year to year with the federal interest rate. If interest rates go down, the mortgage interest rate goes down; if interest rates rise, the mortgage interest rate rises, as well. On most VRMs, the interest rate can jump up to 1 percent per year for five years. So, if you got a VRM at 8 percent and interest rates rose every year, at the end of five years you would have a 13 percent interest rate. Also known as *adjustable-rate mortgage*.

Things to Check Out Before You Buy

THERE ARE MANY THINGS to consider when buying a house. The following list of topics is not intended to be comprehensive, but it does offer a good starting point for new home buyers. As you work through the topics, don't allow yourself to become overly anxious.

Inspections

The best way to be sure that you're getting a good house for your money is to have it inspected by a professional who can look at everything from the basement to the chimney. Many couples wait until after they have made a bid on a home to begin the inspection process, but if there are problems with the house, it could greatly influence your bargaining position, as well as the amount you offer. Finding severe problems could also help you change your mind before it's too late. Seeking professional advice is a good idea for everyone—most couples are so busy figuring out where they'll put the couch or build their workshop that a fair amount of objectivity is lost.

Typically, inspectors charge between $150 and $350 for an inspection, depending on the value of the property. A typical inspection report will include assessments of the plumbing system, kitchen and bathrooms, heating and cooling systems, electrical system, exterior of the house, foundation, structure, yard, roof, chimneys, and crawl space or basement. Specialized tests, such as tests for radon, carbon dioxide, and lead, cost extra.

When looking for an inspector, it's best to avoid one who is recommended by the Realtor you're working with. Chances are, any professional inspector will be unbiased, but for your own peace of mind, it's best to find one who is far removed from negotiations over the house. Look in the *Yellow Pages* under "Building Inspectors" or "Real Estate Inspectors."

Also, when you're walking through a house with an inspector, ask some questions, like why copper piping is so great. You're paying for his or her time anyway, so why not use it wisely? Finally, be wary of an inspector who identifies a problem and then offers his or her services as contractor to fix it. Such an offer would represent a serious conflict of interest.

Heating

Another thing to check out thoroughly when looking for a house is heating. Whether you're talking gas vs. electric appliances, or gas vs. electric heat, the story is the same: gas is cheaper and more efficient. On average, gas appliances and gas heat are less costly to operate. Here are the types of heating systems that are currently available, and the advantages and disadvantages of each.

- **Forced air.** Forced-air is the most cost-effective heating system. A fan in your furnace blows hot air through a series of ducts to all the rooms in the house. Because air is constantly blowing through the system, the filters have to be changed regularly. Also, hot air doesn't always make it to the room at the end of the duct. Installing an in-duct booster fan may help. For $25 or so, the fan will pull heat toward the problem area.

- **Electric.** Because it is more costly than gas heat, electric heat should be avoided, if possible. If you are looking at a home with electric heat, see if the seller is willing to pay for the gas conversion. If not, walk away.

- **Gravity feed.** Probably one of the least effective heating methods, a gravity feed furnace system looks just like a forced air furnace, but relies on gravity to push hot air up to the rooms above. If you've ever been in a house with a gravity feed furnace during the winter, the temperature on the main floor is tropical, the second floor, polar. Some homeowners have installed electric heat on the second floor to compensate for this temperature gap, but that's a double whammy when the bill comes. In-duct boosting fans can improve the circulation of warm air. A gravity feed system has certain advantages: because it doesn't rely on a fan to blow heat, it uses less energy, won't blow dust around, and requires fewer filters.

- **Wood-burning stoves.** Almost twice as efficient as fireplaces, wood-burning stoves create a great deal of heat and are fairly inexpensive to operate when using coal or wood as a fuel source. The downside is the pollution they create. In some areas with a high concentration of homes that burn wood and coal, lawmakers are drafting legislation to regulate their use.

- **Pellet stoves.** Relatively new on the scene, pellet stoves look very much like wood-burning stoves, but, instead of wood, they burn brown pellets that look like rabbit food. Pellet stoves have the efficiency of wood-burning stoves, but without the smoke and pollution. The downside is that the pellets are more expensive than wood or coal.
- **Steam heat.** Steam heat forces steam through radiators located throughout the house. This tends to be relatively efficient, and it can add moisture to the air. People living in steam-heated homes claim to suffer fewer winter colds.
- **Oil furnace.** Much like a forced air furnace, oil furnaces force hot air through ducts, but instead of using gas or electricity, they burn oil. Oil furnaces are slightly more expensive to operate than natural gas, but considerably less expensive than electricity.

Heating is important if you live in the northern part of the world. If you live in the South, check out the cooling system. Are there window air conditioners or central air? How much does it cost to keep the house cool? Are there ceiling fans to keep the cool air circulating? Can you block off rooms you don't use to lower the cost of cooling?

Crib Notes

Tip #30. Talk to the neighbors.

This is where you will be living, so go visit with the neighbors to see what they are like. Drive by at various times of the day. The house may look peaceful and tranquil at noon, but is it quiet on a Friday night? Sunday afternoon?

Tip #31. Check out the school system.

Schools are rated according to academic levels, sports, and so forth. Unless you plan on selling in a few years, this should be a major consideration.

Tip #32. Avoid houses that are "just the right size."

Even if you have no other kids, "just the right size" can quickly become "too crowded." If you must buy a smaller house, leave yourself with options: a basement that can be finished, an attic that can be converted to a bedroom, a porch that can be enclosed, and so forth.

Tip #33. Remember, empty houses look bigger than they really are.

Take measurements and make sure that all of your belongings will fit comfortably. Pay particular attention to specific spaces for refrigerators, microwaves, and so forth.

Tip #34. Beware of the enhancements.

At open houses, Realtors will often add certain features to make a house seem more homey—a roaring fire in the fireplace, the smell of fresh-baked bread wafting from the kitchen, a touch of vanilla extract rubbed on light bulbs throughout the house to add a certain ambiance.... These things are fine, but don't let them cloud your judgment.

Resources

Books

Eldred, Gary W. *The 106 Common Mistakes Homebuyers Make (And How to Avoid Them)*. New York: John Wiley & Sons, 1998.

Glink, Ilyce R. *10 Steps To Home Ownership: A Workbook for First-Time Buyers*. New York: Times Books, 1996.

Glink, Ilyce R. *100 Questions Every First-Time Home Owner Should Ask: With Answers from Top Brokers Around the Country*. New York: Times Books, 1994.

Godfrey, Neale S., and Tad Richards. *From Cradle to College*. New York: Harper Business, 1997.

Irwin, Robert. *The Home Inspection Troubleshooter*. Chicago: Dearborn Publishing, 1995.

Irwin, Robert. *Tips And Traps When Buying A Home*. New York: McGraw-Hill, 1997.

Organizations

U.S. Department of Housing and Urban Development
7th and D St., SW
Washington, DC 20410-3000
For information on FHA mortgage insurance, write for the *Guide to Single Family Home Mortgage Insurance*.

Fannie Mae Customer Education Group
3900 Wisconsin Ave., NW
Washington, DC 20016-2899
Write for the free pamphlet, *A Guide to Home Ownership*.

HSH Associates, Financial Publishers
Dept. FTB
1200 Route 23
Butler, NJ 07405
1-800-873-2837
Publishes *Affording Your First Home,* a pamphlet that contains a review of buyer fees, an amortization table, and financial worksheets.

FmHA
Public Information Center
South Agriculture Building
Independence Avenue Between 12th and 14th Streets, SW
Washington, D.C. 20250
(202) 720-4323
The Farmers Home Administration has a program of no-money-down mortgages for moderate-income families that buy in a rural area. Write for information.

The American Society of Home Inspectors (ASHI)
85 West Algonquin Road
Arlington Heights, IL 60005
(847) 290-1920
Write for a list of member inspectors in your area.

✍ WRAP UP ✌

And in the end I realized that I took more than I gave.
That I was trusted more than I trusted.
That I was loved more than I loved.
That what I was looking for was not to be found, but to be made.
—She's Having a Baby

fter the publication of *Crib Notes for the First Year of Marriage: A Survival Guide for Newlyweds*, I became a household name. Of course, it was only within my own household that I was well known, but I looked it up, and that still counts. The first Crib Notes book was well received, fun to write, and fun to promote.

One short promotional trip was a book signing in Rochester, New York, which is only about three hours from our home. Since Debbie was expecting Alex in a few months and it would probably be the last opportunity to get away for a while, we took Nick and made a long weekend out of it. After the book signing, I went back to the hotel to get Debbie and Nick so we could meet some friends for dinner.

Under normal conditions Nick is great at restaurants. But that day had been exciting, and, instead of sleeping in the car, he'd spent the entire trip rocking in the car seat, burying himself in toys, and telling us the story about the monkey dog lady that lollipops the juice boy. (I'm currently helping him put it into script form, and we're pitching it to the networks.) In any event, demonic forces were building inside of Nick, ready to slowly take control of his body and mind and spread terror in the hearts of all mortals who opposed him. In other words, he was going to be a real pill.

Since our friends, Susan and Eddie, had four kids themselves, and we had Nicholas, the Dark Lord of the Underworld, we decided to go someplace kid-friendly, eat fast, and get out of there before the insurance people could properly assess the damages. When you're looking for a restaurant that's kid-friendly, you need high chairs, booster chairs, place mats you can color on, salty microwaved food that has no nutritional value, a good first-aid department, two fire extinguishers, and flare guns stationed throughout the room.

So we went to a Denny's Restaurant and sat at an intimate table for nine. We got everyone seated, ordered, sat back, and watched Nicholas begin to work the room. Usually, this entails walking from table to table, smiling, introducing himself, and asking for political support if he should decide to run for office. Since this was the no-sleep version of working the room, Nick was demanding money from each table while spinning his head around and avoiding any holy water in the vicinity.

As I watched my wife and Susan visit—as Nick pondered whether to take a traveler's check from table four or hold out for cash—I understood completely. There in the center of Denny's, Eddie and Susan, the super-parents, seemed to enjoy each moment of quiet and each moment of noise, adjusting whenever necessary and savoring that adjustment. And as I leaned back and sipped my coffee, about to be a father for the second time, and about to begin this book, I understood that the key to being a parent is to enjoy all of it, the quiet and the chaos.

The next day, I shared this revelation with Eddie. After a solid minute of confused staring and some questions about whether drug testing was mandatory at my place of employment, he agreed. Eddie and Susan enjoyed being parents, and they were good at it. This didn't mean that life was *Leave It to Beaver;* most of the time, it was more like, "We interrupt this program for a special report." But they enjoyed the mania mixed with the normality.

After this Oracle at Denny's, I accepted that things don't always go according to plan. Sometimes, plans just don't work.

Crib Notes Outtakes

I WAS THINKING the other day about all the bizarre ramblings that never made it into the first Crib Notes book. These were mainly stories, mental wanderings, and goofy stuff—all somewhat interesting, but with no nutritional value whatsoever.

When I tried to include these sections in the first book, my editor would send them back, saying, "Everett, although your story about the cow is amusing, what does it have to do with budgeting?" And another great piece of writing would be lost forever.

In the same way, I wanted to create a chapter for some of the goofier stuff I found while writing this book. Much of it is mindless trivia, most having very little to do with fatherhood, but I didn't want to throw it out. In this chapter I've found a home for almost everything—except the cows.

Now, cows have an important place in a book about the first year of fatherhood, since "moo" is usually the very first animal sound we make to encourage our babies to speak (after "dada"). Hopefully, this argument will be strong enough to convince my editor to allow these few paragraphs to remain in the book.

Cows

My friend hit a cow. She says it jumped out in front of her car, and she couldn't stop. It's lucky she didn't get hurt, which is more than I can say for the cow and the car, but still, the event raises some questions that need to be answered. Why did the slowest moving land mammal jump out in front of her car? What was that cow thinking? Was the cow escaping to the city, off to find a better life? Was the cow at the end of her rope, unable to take the pressures of dairy life? I guess we'll never know.

Here's another cow story: Last summer, there was a horrific crime—a drive-by shooting—that hit the news for several weeks. In our little corner of the world, drive-by shootings are unheard of, but what really made this story bizarre was that the victims of this crime were two cows.

At four o'clock one morning, two cows were gunned down by unidentified assailants using automatic weapons. I have looked into this matter and come up with a few theories.

1. Those cows knew something. Oh, they looked like clean-cut bovines, but they were involved in something dirty and got in way over their heads.

2. The cows were participating in The Witness Relocation Program. They were really sheep that turned state's witness against various farm crime bosses, in exchange for complete immunity and a new identity. They had been living quiet lives as cows until they were finally exposed and eliminated.

3. The chickens snuffed the cows. On the surface, everything looked fine, but those seemingly harmless chickens had been envious of the cows for years, and everyone knew it. They waited until the right time came, then did the dirty deed.

4. It's possible that Cletus and Bobby Thugson got liquored up one night, and decided to go shoot something.

This case is currently being investigated. We'll get more information to you as it becomes available.

Chinese Birth Chart

The following is a Chinese birth chart. Supposedly, it was buried in a Beijing tomb for 700 years. The original is in the Institute of Science in Beijing. The chart is supposed to be 99 percent accurate in predicting the sex of your unborn child (it was 50 percent with us). Just go straight across the top of the chart until you come to the month the child was conceived, then run your finger down to the age of the mother when she will give birth.

	J	F	M	A	M	Jn	Ju	A	S	O	N	D
18	F	M	F	M	M	M	M	M	M	M	M	M
19	M	F	M	F	F	M	M	F	M	M	F	F
20	F	M	F	M	M	M	M	M	M	F	M	M
21	M	F	F	F	F	F	F	F	F	F	F	F
22	F	M	M	F	M	F	F	M	F	F	F	F
23	M	M	M	F	M	M	F	F	F	M	M	F
24	M	F	F	M	M	F	M	F	M	M	F	M
25	F	M	F	M	F	M	F	M	F	M	M	M
26	M	M	M	M	M	F	M	F	F	M	F	F
27	F	F	M	M	F	M	F	F	M	F	M	M
28	M	M	M	F	F	M	F	M	F	F	M	F
29	F	M	F	F	M	F	F	M	F	M	F	F
30	M	M	F	M	F	M	M	M	M	M	M	M
31	M	M	M	M	F	F	M	F	M	F	F	F
32	M	F	F	M	F	M	M	F	M	M	F	M
33	F	M	M	F	F	M	F	M	F	M	M	F
34	M	M	F	F	M	F	M	M	F	M	F	F
35	M	F	M	F	M	F	M	F	M	M	F	M
36	M	F	M	M	M	F	M	M	F	F	F	F
37	F	F	M	F	F	F	M	F	F	M	M	M
38	M	M	F	F	M	F	F	M	F	F	M	F
39	F	F	M	F	F	F	M	F	M	M	F	M
40	M	M	M	F	M	F	M	F	M	F	F	M
41	F	F	M	F	M	M	F	F	M	F	M	F
42	M	F	F	M	M	M	M	F	M	F	M	M
43	F	M	F	F	M	M	M	F	F	F	M	M
44	M	F	F	F	M	F	M	M	F	M	F	M

Predictions

- There is a 70 percent chance that you will pose your sleeping child with a pair of glasses, a hat, or some other prop, and then take a picture.
- There is a 98 percent chance that your child's first Halloween costume will resemble a pumpkin.
- There is a 75 percent chance that you will take pictures of your child on the potty, and then show people.
- There is a 46 percent chance that you will drink some baby formula, just to see what it tastes like.
- There is a 56 percent chance that you will put cereal in the formula a month before the doctor recommends it.
- There is an 86 percent chance that you will be the disciplinarian rather than your wife, because you have the deeper voice.

What I Learned from Nick and Alex (from Birth to Age Three)

- Yellow, green, blue, and red Play Doh, when mixed together, make a blackish-brown color.
- The disk drive of a computer is the perfect size to accommodate an unwrapped slice of processed cheese.
- After watching *The Lion King* for the forty-seventh time, a toddler may become bored with it.
- Cats do not like being held by their tails.
- Disney films are only fun if you own every tie-in action figure, coloring book, toy, and sticker ever made.
- Across a crowded room, a baby of three months can tell the difference between peaches and peas.
- A three-year-old can spot a piece of candy no bigger than a dime from three hundred yards away on a cloudy day.
- The water left in a cigar humidor acts as a laxative if you drink it.
- A lady named Doris works weekends at the Poison Control Center. She's very nice.
- Once you become a parent, Barney becomes less annoying.
- Babies should not be given peas just before they sneeze.

- Driveways are conducive to sleep. Don't believe me? Drive a thousand miles with a screeching child, then pull into your own driveway.
- Legos will pass through the digestive system of a three-year-old.
- French fries are a desired food group at any time of the day.
- A baby of three months can hold two-and-a-half pounds of food under the folds of his or her chin.
- A parent can understand his or her own two-year-old child's words, but not another two-year-old's.
- A teething child can scream as loudly as the entire Zulu nation.
- The sound of a wooden spoon being banged against a pot becomes annoying after four seconds.
- Mommy and Daddy's bed is the best place to sleep.
- Swear words are the easiest ones for a toddler to pronounce.
- A flashlight, dropped down a heating duct, will remain on for nine hours before going dead.
- A human being can go for three days on three hours of sleep. After that, everything turns a milky blue color.
- Basset hounds do not enjoy being placed in the baby jumper seat.
- A one-year-old knows what McDonald's is, even if he or she has never been there before.

Fathers' Thumbs Up To . . .

- Stores that have changing tables in their men's restrooms.
- The guy who designed the television remote control. Channel surfing is the only way I stayed awake during those late night feedings.
- The guys who designed SmartPlay and the other play areas where the parents can go in with the kids. No longer do we need to say, "Oh, man, why didn't they have this when I was a kid?" Even my friends without kids want to go to the playland; when things get tight financially, I rent Nick out to them, and they thank me for it.

A Father's Calorie Counter

During the First Year of Fatherhood

- Putting the baby in the car seat and driving around the block so the baby will stop crying and finally go to sleep.

  +345 calories (The Dunkin Donuts drive-thru is open all night.)

- Giving the baby a bath.

  -34 calories

- Cleaning up after the bath.

  -156 calories

- Showing the baby's picture to someone at work.

  -25 calories

- Winding up the baby swing.

  -2 calories

- Baby's first words.

  -345 calories (Running to get the camcorder to record it, and then trying to get the baby on the phone to say the words to your mother.)

After the First Year of Fatherhood

- Playing horsey.

  -124 calories

- Giving a toddler a bath.

  -27 calories

- Chasing a naked toddler through the house, trying to dry the child off and get his or her pajamas on.

  -134 calories

- Trying to fish your car keys from the bottom of the heating duct.

  -87 calories

- Watching your child go up to Mr. Plotchins and ask him where his tail is, " 'Cause Daddy says you're a jackass."

  -456 calories (The sweat alone can be as much as 200 calories.)

- Taking a feather duster, sticking it in the back of your pants, and clucking like a chicken, while your three-year-old chases you with a fishing net.

  Not sure how many calories. (Debbie always makes me stop and take a nap, so I can never measure it accurately.)

The World According to Nicholas: A Three-Year-Old's View of Parenting Roles

- It's Mommy's job to play farm with me (I like to make her be the chicken).
- It's Daddy's job to be my horse and let me ride him around until he has no feeling left in his lower body.

- It's Mommy's job to hold me when I'm sad.
- It's Daddy's job to bring me some juice while Mommy is holding me when I'm sad.

- It's Mommy's job to send me to the time-out chair.
- It's Daddy's job to make sure I stay there.

- It's Mommy's job to stop cooking and play with me.
- It's Daddy's job to buy take-out so Mommy can stop cooking and play with me.

- It's Mommy's job to say no.
- It's Daddy's job to say no really loud, so I know it's not a drill.

- It's Daddy's job to dress me.
- It's Mommy's job to dress me so I match.

- It's Mommy's job to take my temperature.
- It's Daddy's job to watch her take my temperature.

- It's Daddy's job to make the stuffed animals dance and sing "Crocodile Rock."
- It's Mommy's job to use cookie cutters on my bologna so I can have stars and bunnies for lunch.

In addition to these roles, there are certain rituals we have established. Let's say, for example, that I'm being a bad father and won't let Nick put the cat in the toilet. He'll stick out his lower lip, slump his shoulders, and slink off, gloomily exclaiming, "I'm sad." Sometimes, if I'm being really cruel to him, he'll use the even stronger version: "You make me sad."

Often, though, I am not the cause of his distress. That's when he'll walk in and say, "I'm sad, Daddy." And I'll carry him into the other room to see if a crayon broke; or Bee-Baa, his imaginary friend, has hurt his feelings; or the lamp made him sad; or the curtains won't talk to him. I'll get Bee-Baa on the phone, scold the lamp, or tickle the curtains, and after a few moments, Nick's as good as new. Once again, I end up with a happy, content child, or the makings of an evil criminal genius, which makes me proud either way.

The Last Nick Story

WHEN NICK WAS TWO, every time anyone left the house, he'd say, "Don't hit the mouse." We used to question this, trying to figure out what he meant. What mouse? How would we hit it? But he'd only answer back, "Drive on the grass, and don't hit the mouse." After a while, we translated this to mean, "Be careful. Good luck, and keep in touch."

As you finish your first year of fatherhood, you'll have a million such stories, and you'll have changed a million ways from the person you were a year ago. That is part of the gift.

So congratulations, again. Congratulations on being a new father and a new person. Congratulations on the opportunity to see the universe all over again, for the first time. Congratulations on the excitement of beginning your new life and new family.

And remember, whatever you do, drive on the grass, and don't hit the mouse.

Crib Notes for After the First Year

Tip #35. Be sure you know the consequences of getting down on your hands and knees.

This is the universal signal that your child should call all of his or her friends, jump on your back, and make you play horsey all the way to the mall.

Tip #36. Get a big toy box and little toy box.

If you get a shallow plastic tote for small toys and another one for the larger ones, you'll save yourself an enormous amount of grief when you need to find Barbie's left shoe or Buzz Lightyear's rocket pack.

Tip #37. Use a timer.

Kids have no comprehension of "later," "in a while," or "in ten minutes." We use a wind-up egg timer. When this goes off, it's time to come in, go to bed, or take a nap. Nick understands this.

Tip #38. Buy only washable crayons and markers.

Even though your children would *never* write on the wall or floor, it's better to be safe. These crayons and markers wash out of clothes and tablecloths, and are easy to remove from hands and faces.

Tip #39. Beware of the red dye.

Some children are sensitive to the red dyes found in food. This dye is in everything, from Children's Tylenol to cake frosting. If your child is having trouble falling asleep or is sometimes hyperactive, check the environment for red dye.

ABOUT THE AUTHOR

by Nick De Morier

I speak for my brother, Alex, when I say that we would like to set some things straight regarding this book and our father. First of all, our image throughout this publication was not always portrayed in the most positive manner. We would have our attorneys look into this, except that every time I try to call, my dad offers me a Snickers bar to get off the phone, and things get a little fuzzy after that. So, in lieu of the $19 million we were seeking in punitive damages, we've settled for the opportunity to write this section of the book and talk about him for a while.

Our father is a somewhat goofy-looking guy who gets up very early in the morning to write, and he does this until my brother Alex demands that he stop. (This used to be my job, but as a three-year-old, I need to focus on bigger things; I have passed the scepter on to him.) Our father is a writer and lecturer, although the idea of someone actually paying him to talk is completely beyond Alex and me, our mother, our grandparents, and Mrs. Parker, who lives across the street. My father has written several magazine articles and a book titled *Crib*

Notes for the First Year of Marriage: A Survival Guide for Newlyweds. He embarrasses us at family functions, the same way he did on CNN, the Fox News Network, and all the radio programs he's been on.

The author tends to have baby vomit on his shoulder for hours without knowing it, and when he's lost something, he always finds the thing he was looking for the last time he couldn't find something. Although my mother is perfect in every way, our dad has several key areas to work on. We're trying to be patient. You can e-mail him, if you like, at EVdemorier@aol.com, but there is no guarantee that I won't shut the computer off while he's answering you. I tend to do that when I'm being ignored.

❧ INDEX ❧